The Con

Contract Law

A Civilized Approach to the Law

The Compact Guide to Contract Law

A Civilized Approach to the Law

Jefferson Hane Weaver

Attorney at Law

WEST PUBLISHING COMPANY

St. Paul New York Los Angeles San Francisco

Composition by Parkwood Composition Services
Copyediting by Julie Bach
Cover Image by Lee Sievers
Cover Design by Kristin Weber

50 W. Kellogg Boulevard
P.O. Box 64526
St. Paul, MN 55164-1003

Printed in United States of America
97 96 95 94 93 92 91 90 8 7 6 5 4 3 2 1 0

Library of Congress Cataloging-in-Publication Data

Weaver, Jefferson Hane
The Compact Guide to Contract Law: A Civilized Approach to the Law / Jefferson Hane Weaver
p. cm.
Includes index.
ISBN 0-314-68767-X
1. Contracts—United States I. Title
KF801.Z9W38 1990
346.73'02—dc20 89-28671
[347.3062] CIP

This book is dedicated to
Mark Christopher Louis Weaver,
Catharine Emily Hane Weaver,
and their beautiful mother,
Shelley Jo Weaver

About the Author

Jefferson Hane Weaver received his B. A. from the University of North Carolina at Chapel Hill, and his J.D. from the Columbia University School of Law in New York City. He also received his M. A. and his M. Phil. from the Columbia University Graduate School of Arts and Sciences, where he is now completing his Ph.D. He has written *The World of Physics* (3 volumes), and with Lloyd Motz has written *The Concepts of Science, The Story of Physics, The Atomic Scientists*, and *The Unfolding Universe*. He currently practices law in Fort Lauderdale, Florida, where he resides with his wife, Shelley Jo, and their two children, Mark Christopher Louis and Catharine Emily Hane.

CONTENTS

Foreword

When one begins to write a book about the law, it is often difficult, if not impossible, to say something new, because so many earlier writers have dealt with similar topics, often with greater competence or depth. Even though there are a number of "how to" books about the law that are purportedly geared toward the general audience, they are primarily "practical guides," such as how to write a will without a lawyer or how to avoid probate or form a corporation. There do not appear to be many books available to the wider audience that discuss the intellectual foundations of the law in a manner that is both accessible and entertaining.

My primary reason for writing this book on contract law was to provide a straightforward explanation of the subject while having some fun with the examples used to illustrate particular points or concepts. A discussion does not have to be dusty or ponderous for it to be valuable, but the subject must be treated with respect or else readers may lose any initial enthusiasm they might have had for the subject.

The scope of this book is necessarily limited to the basic features of contract law. I have touched upon some aspects of sales law where appropriate, but I have not treated sales law separately (even though such an approach is advisable) as I found that much of it would be repetitive or overly detailed. Bearing in mind that this book is geared toward the general audience and not lawyers, I have tried to present the subject in as simple and uncomplicated a manner as possible without compromising its integrity.

A summary of a subject is not a wellspring of originality, because it tries to explain what is already known. The originality of this book stems more from its form and style of presentation than its content. This book owes a great intellectual debt to a number of earlier works about contract law. These books helped me to crystallize and organize my own thoughts and writing. Consequently, I would like to acknowledge the following books, which proved to be of invaluable assistance in formulating the structure and content of this book: William E. Burby, *Law Refresher: Contracts*, 4th ed. St. Paul: West Publishing Co., 1971; Joseph Chitty, *Chitty on Contracts*, 23rd ed. London: Sweet & Maxwell, 1968 (2 vols); William Lawrence Clark, *Handbook of the Law of Contracts*, 4th ed. Ed. by Archibald H. Throckmorton and Alvin C. Brightman. St. Paul: West Publishing Co., 1931; William George Henry Cook, *Elements of the Law of Contracts*. London: Butterworth & Co., 1931; Andrew Joseph Coppola, *The Law of Business Contracts*. New York: John Wiley, 1964; Arthur Linton Corbin, *Corbin on Contracts*. St. Paul: West Publishing Co., 1952; Monroe H. Freedman, *Cases and Materials on Contracts*. St. Paul: West Publishing Co., 1973; Charles Fried, *Contract as Promise: A Theory of Contractual*

Obligation. Cambridge: Harvard University Press, 1982; David P. Gauthier, *Morals By Agreement.* Oxford: Clarendon Press, 1986; Harold Canfield Havighurst, *The Nature of Private Contract.* Evanston, Ill.: Northwestern University Press, 1961; Denis J. Kennan, *Objective Tests in the Law of Contract.* London: Pitman, 1973; Ian R. Macneil, *The New Social Contract: An Inquiry into Modern Contractual Relations.* New Haven: Yale University Press, 1980; Howard B. Miller and Michael S. Josephson, *Contracts.* Culver City, Calif.: Josephson/Kluwer Legal Educational Centers, Inc., 1986; Grace Powers Monaco, *Outline on Contracts.* Irvington-on-Hudson, New York: American Legal Publications, 1968; Addison Mueller and Arthur I. Rosett, *Contract Law and Its Application.* Mineola, New York: Foundation Press, 1971; John Edward Murray, *Cases and Materials on Contracts.* Indianapolis: Bobbs-Merrill, 1969; Gordon D. Schaber and Claude D. Rohwer, *Contracts in a Nutshell.* St. Paul: West Publishing Co., 1975; Laurence Packer Simpson, *Handbook on the Law of Contracts*, 2nd ed. St. Paul: West Publishing Co., 1965; Edward Ludwig Teller, *Law of Contracts.* New York: Harmon Publications, 1948; G. H. Treitel, *An Outline of the Law of Contract.* London: Butterworths, 1975; Samuel Williston, *A Treatise on the Law of Contracts*, 3rd ed. by Walter H. E. Jaeger, Mt. Kisco, New York: Baker, Voorhis, 1957; Richard Wincor, *Contracts in Plain English.* New York: McGraw-Hill, 1976.

Jefferson Hane Weaver
February 18, 1989

CHAPTER 1

The Elements of a Contract

I knew a very wise man so much of Sir Christopher's sentiment, that he believed that if a man were permitted to make all the ballads, he need not care who should make the laws of a nation.

— Andrew Fletcher
of Saltoun

1

Preliminary Considerations

What is a contract? Some would argue that it is an instrument by which the more enterprising people in the world are able to bilk the rest of us of our savings. Others would say it is a two-syllable word beginning with the third letter of our alphabet. Still others would say nothing because they believe contracts have an almost mystical quality about them; this reverence may be similar to the awe that was felt when a loaf of bread was first cut into sixteen even slices. Finally, there are those who would not care very much about the question at all, but would prefer to watch their game shows.

What is a contract? Is it an obligation? A duty? A right? An agreement? The envelope, please. A contract is an enforceable agreement between two or more parties that creates obligations to perform or not to perform specified acts. A contract may be expressly created by a promise or set of promises between the parties in oral or written form or it may

be implied when an agreement is manifested by the conduct of the parties. In a properly drafted contract, the responsibilities of each of the parties is clearly described. By using a contract, any natural person or other legal entity such as a corporation can establish a legally binding relationship with any other party.

What is crucial to the understanding of contract law is that something of value must be given for the contract to be enforceable. Value is not limited to money but can include any right one party may exercise against the other, such as the right to collect a debt or to compel performance of a particular act. In any event, the value must be given in exchange for the promise to support a binding contract. Lawyers use the word "consideration" to denote value. When we say that a contract must be supported by consideration in order for it to be valid, we mean that some benefit or some burden must be given or assumed in order for the contract to be enforceable.

Contracts express what are called expectation values; each party expects to derive a certain benefit from the contract and agrees to incur some obligation or cost in order to obtain that benefit. When one party fails to live up to the terms of the contract, the other party can try to protect its expectation interest by suing to collect the benefit that it would have received had the contract been performed. This legal remedy enables injured parties to recover the benefit they bargained for under the contract or, if that is no longer possible, to be put back in the same position they occupied before making the contract. If you offer to sell me a flatulent songbird for seventy dollars and I accept your offer (perhaps because I have a cold that week), your expectation interest (the benefit you expect to receive under the contract) is the sale price and my expectation interest is the songbird. If you change your mind, I could sue you to make you give the songbird to me. This contractual remedy is known as specific performance. My forcing you to give me the bird in exchange for my payment of the seventy dollars would protect my expectation interest in the contract.

On the other hand, if we both performed our obligations under the contract but the songbird died ten minutes later of tuberculosis, I could sue you for the return of my seventy dollars because I had not received the benefit of the bargain—a healthy songbird. By getting my money back, I would be put back in my original position and the contract would no longer be in effect. If my malodorous songbird flourished, however, and I recovered from my cold and discovered its talent for air pollution, I would not be able to argue that I did not receive my expectation interest in the contract. I had ample opportunity to inspect the bird and examine its flaws before I made the purchase. I should have been able to ascertain exactly what I was buying; the fact that I could not detect my new pet's unique scent was due to my own illness and not to any attempt by you to conceal the more disagreeable aspects of its personality.

Because many disputes arise between parties to a contract as to their respective rights and obligations, the first step any court reviewing a contract must take is to decide whether in fact an enforceable contract was actually formed. Only after the court decides that a contract does exist will it then evaluate the claims of the respective parties. The court must first decide if the parties gave their mutual assent to the terms of the agreement which formed the contract. Mutual assent simply means that both parties did in fact agree to the same thing at the same time. This "meeting of the minds" usually follows negotiations between the parties. These negotiations typically are initiated when one party makes an offer and are concluded when the other party accepts it.

Determining whether there was a subjective meeting of the minds is often difficult. For that reason, the court will resort to an objective standard based on the apparent intentions each party manifested to the other. In other words, did the parties act in such a way that an observer could reasonably conclude that they both agreed to the same terms and conditions? There is no mutual assent if I offer to sell you a widget that I know to be a mechanical device and you reasonably believe to be an item of clothing. We both have a different object in mind so there is no agreement about the subject matter of the contract. Because the court cannot read our minds, however, it would look for evidence to show that we were contracting for completely different objects.

The same principle holds true with respect to the basic terms and conditions of a contract. Stubbornly insisting on interpretating contractual terms in a manner radically different from the rest of the world is not a good way to get out of a contract. You should be forewarned that a court will decide whether your interpretation of a term is reasonable under the circumstances. If you purchase a new car but find that no spare tire was included in the trunk, you would certainly be able to argue that your purchase was made with a reasonable belief that a spare would be included. On the other hand, if you were a gangster who needed a spacious trunk for storing bodies, then you might not even want to have a spare tire included in the deal. Consequently, you might have no expectation that a spare tire would be sold with the car, even though your attitude would be contrary to the views of the vast majority of automobile drivers.

Another example may better illustrate this point. If you complain that your dashboard was fitted in vinyl and not teak, a court would not likely find in your favor and order that the vinyl be replaced because a teak dashboard is not found in most automobiles. Of course, if you had bought an exotic car that was *supposed* to include a teak dashboard, then your reasonable expectation would not have been met under the contract and a court would rule in your favor.

The basic terms of the contract must be clearly specified before the parties can be said to have come to a mutual agreement. This requirement does not mean that every single clause of the contract must be spelled out in painstaking detail, but only that the terms that form the basis of the agreement must be unequivocal. Although some lawyers would be perfectly happy to draft five-hundred page contracts to govern every consumer transaction such as the purchase of a gallon of bleach or a package of cotton swabs, to do so would be horribly expensive and unnecessarily detailed. An ambiguous term will not necessarily cause a court to strike down a contract because public policy favors contracts. A court will resolve the ambiguity in the contract by referring to any subsequent acts or agreements that help to show what the parties might have intended with respect to the ambiguous term.

The failure of a sales contract to specify one or more basic terms will not invalidate the contract. An unclear or open term can be determined in several ways. First, the court will look to the "course of performance" between the parties, or the past actions of the parties. (What did the parties do?) If the course of performance is of little help in filling in the missing terms, the court will then turn to the "course of dealing" and try to decide what the parties actually meant when they were dealing with each other. (What was the intent of the parties?) If this strategy fails to shed any light, the court will resort to "trade usage" to clarify an unclear or ambiguous term and will refer to particular customs and practices in that business. (What does "timely delivery" mean in the shoe business?) In any event, the court must find that the parties did intend to come to an agreement, and that there is some way in which an appropriate remedy can be fashioned. If not, the contract will fail.

To be enforceable a contract must specify a quantity. If no quantity is specified, a legally-enforceable agreement cannot be said to exist because it is unenforceable. If I agree to sell you "some" pickles and I fail to carry out my promise, you cannot enforce the promise because I did not specify the quantity of pickles that I was willing to sell. If I had said "one barrel of pickles," a court would find the quantity sufficiently definite to order me to perform my part of the agreement or to assess money damages if I am unable to deliver the barrel of pickles as agreed. A quantity term is even more important than a price term because the price may be inferred by referring to the market price of the product that existed when the contract was formed. By contrast, a quantity term cannot be inferred from a price term unless the price gives some indication as to the quantity of goods envisioned by the contract. For example, if a contract called for "$20 worth of pickles," a quantity could be inferred by looking at how many pickles could be bought for twenty dollars at the time of the agreement.

For a contract to be binding, it must be supported by consideration. This means that one party promises to do something in exchange for a promise by the other party to confer some benefit. For example, "I promise to board your bloodthirsty pet dog while you visit your relatives in exchange for your promise to pay me fifty dollars for taking care of your pet." Even though I might not like your dog, our agreement (though oral) is enforceable. I have assumed the burden of boarding the dog in reliance on your promise to pay me for my services and emergency room visits when you return. This contract is known as a "bilateral contract" because it involves the exchange of promises between the contracting parties. I promise not to kill your dog while you are away in exchange for your promise to pay me for serving as a chew toy.

A "unilateral contract," by contrast, is the exchange of a promise for the performance itself and not the promise to perform. In other words, I can accept your promise to pay me ten dollars for painting the shutters of your house only when I begin to perform the task itself. In the case of a unilateral contract, I would not be promising to perform but instead indicating my reliance on your promise by actually beginning to paint the shutters or at least scattering a lot of buckets, brushes, cans, and drop cloths around your front yard.

The parties to a contract are required to exercise "good faith" in the performance of their obligations or duties. Good faith does not require that the parties be candidates for sainthood. Good faith means only that the parties try to complete their respective responsibilities under the contract to the best of their abilities. This obligation to exercise good faith cannot be avoided or waived; a court will imply such a duty with respect to all the parties. If one party conducts itself in a manner that clearly shows bad faith (the party never intended to perform its part of the contract) then that party may not be given the benefit of the doubt if a conflict arises as to the meaning of a term or condition of the contract. A sales contract made by a merchant must meet a test of good faith and show that the merchant has observed reasonable commercial standards of fair dealing in that particular trade or business. We impose a higher standard of care on a merchant than a casual buyer or seller, just as we impose a higher standard of care on a medical specialist than on a general practicioner.

The Offer

A contract usually originates when an offer is made by one party to another. The offer specifies the terms on which the offering party (the offeror) is willing to enter into a contractual relationship. By making this offer, the offeror creates in the other party (the offeree) the right to accept the offer and form a contract. The offeree only has to accept the terms of the offer to create a valid contract. However, this right of acceptance is not unlimited; it must be shown in both the language of the offer and its context that the offeror intended to be legally bound by the offeree's acceptance of the offer. The test is whether a reasonable person would believe that the statement by the offeror is an actual offer—as opposed to an offer to negotiate—and that only the offeree's assent is necessary to form an agreement.

A statement of my future intentions ("I will sell my cherry wood bureau for $1,000 tomorrow") does not give anyone hearing the statement a right to accept the terms because the context of the statement shows that it is not an actual offer to sell. It is merely an expression of my future plans. I have not created a power of acceptance in any party hearing my statement. Similarly, my request for a price quotation ("Please give me a price for one case of motor oil as I have a date with an auto mechanic") does not give the other party a power of acceptance because it is only a request for information about the product.

Moreover, an invitation to negotiate ("Would you think about buying my affections for one hundred dollars?") is not an offer; no power of acceptance is conferred on the listener because of the indefinite language of the statement. Instead, such a statement invites the listener to negotiate about the terms of the sale. Furthermore, the terms of an offer must be clear and unambiguous ("I offer to sell you two types of affection for seventy-five dollars").

Whether an advertisement aimed at the general public is an offer or simply an invitation to negotiate also depends on whether the language is sufficiently definite to create a power of acceptance in the one seeing the advertisement. Whether this power of acceptance is found depends on whether the advertisement is phrased in the form of a promise and includes a specific quantity term. For example, an advertisement in a store window offering a ten-dollar discount on thermometers normally priced at $23 will not be regarded as an offer but simply a statement of intention or an invitation to negotiate. The language is not couched in the form of a promise and no quantity is specified. If, on the other hand, the store offered the discount to the first ten buyers of that type of thermometer, then an enforceable promise would be found because the language is more definite and a quantity is given. An implicit power of acceptance would be created in the first ten buyers who actually paid for that model of thermometer.

An offer made as a joke may be enforceable if the offeree reasonably believed that it was a genuine offer. My promise to go over Niagara Falls in a barrel if you promise to pay me one hundred dollars would likely be interpreted as a joke unless you could show that it was reasonable to believe that my offer was prompted by my intent to form an agreement. Even if you believe that the world would be a much better place with me bobbing around in the froth underneath Niagara Falls, it is unlikely that you would be able to enforce this agreement owing to its absurd context. However, if I make an offer in jest that otherwise appears to be valid, I may be bound to perform my promise.

The same is true for statements made in anger. The test is whether a reasonable interpretation of the statement shows an intent by the offeror to be bound. However, if you point a gun at me and force me to offer to trade my sports car for your tennis racket, the agreement cannot be enforced because you forced me to make an offer that I would not have otherwise made. I have not voluntarily expressed my intent to be bound. Furthermore, the vast discrepancy in value between the two items would also suggest that the deal was not voluntarily made; it might have been due to an "unconscionable" (ethically or morally intolerable) asymmetry in bargaining power between the parties. Consequently, such a trade would not be enforced by a court.

The person making the offer controls the terms of the offer and decides who may accept the offer. If I offer a fifty dollar reward for the return of my missing show goat, a power of acceptance is created in whomever brings the animal back to me. Even though offers are typically made to one person, the power of acceptance here can be exercised only by the one person who brings the animal back to me. Although I do not know who will collect the reward, I am bound to pay the reward when my goat is returned.

Somewhat different from an advertisement or posted reward is the option contract in which one party pays another party some amount of money to keep an offer open for a fixed amount of time. For example, I might offer to sell my house to you for $100,000. You have always admired my house and believe the asking price to be a bargain. But you are unable and unwilling to pay that price right now because you have to keep moving (you failed to pay a debt you owe to a gangster who does not have a spare tire in his trunk). However, you do not wish to run the risk that I will sell the house to somebody else before you become ready, willing, and able to pay the full price. As a result, you could pay me some agreed amount of money to keep the offer open to you for a specified period of time (the option period) at the $100,000 price until you were ready to pay the full purchase price. In short, you could pay for a right of acceptance, which could be exercised at any time during the option period. If you waited until the day after the option contract expired, however, I would no longer be obligated to sell you the house at that price. The power of acceptance given to you by the option contract would no longer exist since the contract itself would have expired.

The basic terms of any contract must be clear. My promise to pay "some" money to you in exchange for your promise to replace the radiator grille of my station wagon is not definite enough owing to my failure to specify the amount of payment. The basic terms of a contract must be spelled out or else be implied by reference to other parts of the contract or some other standard such as the cost of comparable services. A valid offer should include:

- the names of the parties
- the subject matter
- the time of performance
- and the price.

As noted above, the absence of a basic or "material" term will not defeat the formation of a contract if a court determines that the parties did intend to form a contract and that the missing term can be implied by reference to the language of the contract or other evidence such as the course of performance, the course of dealing, or the trade usage.

The desire of courts to fill the gaps of otherwise valid contracts does not mean that courts will redraft contracts where some of the basic terms are so ambiguous that the intent of the parties cannot be divined. In such a situation, there is no guarantee that a court-drafted contract would necessarily reflect the intentions of the parties. Judges are not mindreaders. Indeed, it is fair to say that the terms of the court-drafted contract might depend more on what the judge ate for breakfast than the actual intention of the parties.

When the contract language is sufficiently clear, however, individual terms such as price, time of delivery, date of delivery, and terms of payment may be implied by reference to existing state statutes that govern commercial transactions. For example, if I neglect to include a price in my offer to sell you eight hundred loaves of bread, a court may order that a reasonable price such as the fair market price at the time of delivery be paid. The same filling-in process is used for most other terms except quantity, the absence of which would prevent the formation of a valid contract.

In requirements contracts and output contracts, however, where a manufacturer offers to supply all the goods a customer may require or a customer promises to purchase all the goods the manufacturer can produce, it is impossible to specify a particular quantity. In such cases, a court will try to determine what amounts are reasonable given the expectations of the contracting parties.

Unexpectedly sudden and significant changes in the quantity demanded or supplied by the parties may make it unfair to continue enforcing the contract. The test is whether the change is so in excess of the parties' original expectations that it would be unconscionable to hold the parties to their original agreement. In such cases, the courts often look to the past course of dealings between the parties to see if the changes are extreme enough to justify striking down the contract. If I am a shoemaker who agrees to sell you all the shoes you require, minor deviations in your requirements from month to month will not prevent the enforcement of our contract. However, if my shoes are very popular with your customers and you decide that you could easily sell five times as many shoes, you will not be able to make a demand on me to increase my production five-fold. Such a change in your requirements would be so great and abrupt that it would be unfair to continue enforcing the contract. Such a level of demand was obviously not contemplated by me when I entered into the original contract.

There are several ways to terminate an offer and thereby extinguish the power of acceptance given to the offeree. I could simply withdraw my offer to sell you my stamp collection before you had exercised your power of acceptance. This action would "revoke" or destroy the offer. No special words or actions are required to revoke an offer; it is enough if the words or conduct (such as sticking out one's tongue and behaving in an obnoxious manner) demonstrate that the offeror no longer intends to give the offeree the power to accept the offer. All offers are revocable except for option contracts (in which money is paid to keep an offer open for a specified time) and certain types of written offers made by merchants.

For the revocation to be effective, it must be received by the offeree. An effective revocation need not be communicated directly to the offeree, however, since the offer could be revoked by the offeror doing something so inconsistent with the terms of the offer that it could no longer be said to exist. If I offer to sell my prized thoroughbred horse to you, I can revoke that offer by selling it to someone else so long as I do so and you find out about the sale before you exercise your power of acceptance. (If you do not learn of my double-dealing until after you have communicated your acceptance, you could argue that I breached a valid contract.) Since I would then no longer have the horse in my possession, a revocation of the offer would be implied. In the case of a unilateral contract where I have promised to pay you one hundred dollars for painting the shutters of my house and your acceptance of this offer will become apparent once you begin work, I can revoke my offer up until the time you start. Once you have begun painting the shutters, however, my power to revoke the offer is extinguished because you have exercised your power of acceptance.

If I make a condition that my offer be accepted within thirty days, then after that period of time has passed, you will no longer have the power to accept its terms. The offeror has absolute discretion to control all of the terms of the offer, including its duration. Failure by the offeree to accept the offer in the specified time causes the offer to lapse regardless of why the offeree chose not to act. When no time limit is given, the courts will ask what would be a reasonable time for an offer of this type to remain open. Reference will be made to such things as prior dealings between the parties, existing business practices, and the type of subject matter involved in deciding how long the contract should be kept open.

An offer may also be revoked if the government passes a law that makes illegal the purpose for which the offer was made. If I promise to pay you $10,000 to print one million bingo cards for me, an act by the state legislature making bingo illegal prior to printing (and thus frustrating the objective of my offer) would revoke the offer. In this example, however, I would have to demonstrate that the bingo cards could not be used for any other legal purpose (such as feeding my show goat), or you would still be able to accept my offer. If I offer to purchase an elephant gun from you and the state legislature then makes the possession of such weapons illegal, the offer would be revoked. There could be no argument about alternative uses for the gun because the legislative act would frustrate the sole purpose of my offer—to possess an enormous gun with which I could intimidate my neighbors.

An offer is also automatically revoked if the subject matter is destroyed before there is a valid acceptance, or if one party dies before the offer has been accepted.

Finally, an offer is terminated if it is rejected by the offeree. The rejection extinguishes the offeree's power to accept the offer. If you reject my offer to sell you a bicycle for fifty dollars, you cannot later accept the offer and demand that I fulfill my promise, because you have already forfeited your power of acceptance. If you instead offer me forty dollars for the bicycle, your offer operates both as a rejection of the original terms of my offer and as a counter-offer by you to buy the bicycle at a lower price. In that case, you confer the power of acceptance on me and I may agree to your terms or reject them outright or make my own counter-offer of some intermediate price such as forty-five dollars and temporary custody of my two bratty nephews who have swarmed in for a weekend visit. As we shall see later, in certain types of sales contracts, the suggestion by one party that new or different terms be included in the agreement does not necessarily terminate the original offer. For our purposes here, however, we should regard a counter-offer as a rejection of the terms of the original offer and instead treat it as a new offer.

Previously we referred to option contracts, which cannot be revoked at the will of the offeror because some form of consideration (value) has been given to keep the offer open for a particular length of time. If the offeror tries to revoke the offer that formed the basis for the option contract (whether by outright withdrawal or by the sale of the subject matter) after being paid by the offeree to keep it open, the offeree can maintain an action for breach of contract since an option contract is legally enforceable.

A "firm" offer is similar to an option contract except that no consideration is required to keep it open. Only merchants can make such offers and these must be written and signed and involve a sale of goods. If no date of expiration is mentioned in the offer, a limit of three months is imposed because it is unfair to continue holding a merchant liable for long periods of time when nothing of value has been given in return.

The Acceptance

After the offer has been made, the offeree must clearly and unambiguously agree to the terms of the offer. The offer must be accepted before the offeree's power of acceptance expires or is otherwise terminated. Whether or not the acceptance actually creates an enforceable contract depends on whether adequate consideration (value) is given. If no benefit is received or no detriment is incurred by either of the parties, then there is no enforceable contract.

Except for the option-contract, which creates a right in its owner that can generally be assigned (transferred) to another party, the power to accept an offer rests exclusively with the offeree. If I offer to sell you my golf clubs for one hundred dollars, for example, your brother has no right to accept my offer and compel me to sell my clubs to him. However, if you paid for an option to buy my golf clubs for one hundred dollars, you could transfer your right to exercise the option to your brother, and he could then enforce the contract and rightfully demand that the clubs be sold to him.

In the case of a store advertisement that promises, for example, to pay $1,000 to the one millionth customer to enter the store, the offeree will not be known until he actually enters the store. As only one person can be the millionth customer, even though his identity is unknown, that person will be able to claim the reward because the power of acceptance has already been conferred on him by the terms of the advertisement. If the person entering the store had no knowledge of the offer being made, however, he would not be able to claim the reward because he did not possess the requisite intent to accept the offer.

A reward may not be accepted by someone whose regular duties include the conduct sought to be induced by the offer. To return to the store example, if the millionth person was not a customer but a police officer or a firefighter responding to an emergency call, the act of entering the store would be in the course of her official duties and not prompted by the advertisement. As a result, she would not be able to claim the reward because she did not incur any legal detriment outside the scope of the duties she was already under a legal duty to perform.

An offeree usually accepts a bilateral contract by giving a promise to perform. The offeror, however, has the power to specify the proper way in which the contract may be accepted. If the offeror requires that acceptance be given in a certain manner, the offeror is not bound if the offer is accepted in any other manner unless he expressly agrees to be bound. If, on the other hand, no manner of acceptance is specified, then the offer may be accepted by the offeree in any reasonable manner. If I offer to sell you a barrel of pickles but require you to respond by telephone call, then your acceptance by mail will not legally bind me. My failure to require a specific form of acceptance would permit you to accept the offer in any similar manner—you could respond by telephone or telegraph or messenger pigeon or fleet-footed goat.

In general, silence on the part of the offeree cannot be construed as an acceptance of an offer. That is because it would be unjust to put a burden on the offeree to respond to an offer in which failure to respond would result in a contract. There are several exceptions to this rule. For example, if the offeror says that the offeree's silence will be interpreted as an acceptance and the offeree remains silent, the offeree has demonstrated the intent to accept the contract. In other words, the offeree's silence is prompted by the intent to accept the contract.

Another exception occurs when two parties have dealt with one another in the past and have previously allowed silence to act as an acceptance in similar transactions. If you have accepted shipments of wool from me in the past by not rejecting them within one week of delivery, then the fact that you do not explicitly reject another shipment of wool within the same time may operate as an acceptance because of our prior dealings. An implied acceptance will also be found when the offeree exercises exclusive dominion over the offeror's property. If I send you a shipment of wool and you do not communicate your acceptance but instead have the wool made into yarn, you have exercised a degree of exclusive control over the wool that is inconsistent with my rights of ownership. Because your actions substantially changed the nature of the good, your acceptance of the wool is implied.

Finally, the recipient of unsolicited goods received through the mail may choose to return the goods to their owner or keep them without obligation. If I mail you a pencil sharpener on my own initiative hoping that you will agree to buy it, you have the option to keep the pencil sharpener or to send it back to me.

In a unilateral contract, the offer can be accepted only by performing in the manner requested by the offeror. In most cases, the offeree does not need to give the offeror notice that such performance has begun unless a substantial period of time has passed since the offer was originally made and it is no longer clear that the offer can still be accepted. If the time between the date of the offer and the beginning of performance is not unreasonable, then the offeree does not need to give notice that performance has begun. However, it is preferable to give notice if only to avoid possible disputes over whether the unilateral contract was actually formed.

In situations where the offer is unclear as to whether a promise to act or the actual performance is required for acceptance, any ambiguity in the language of the offer will be construed against the offeror because the offeror was the one who chose the words used to make the offer. The offeror still has the right to specify the exact manner of acceptance. The strict interpretation of ambiguities against the offeror is intended to put the risk of loss on the one who makes the offer and to protect the good-faith acceptance of the offer by the offeree. When a buyer orders goods but does not specify whether he or she desired the actual shipment of the goods or merely a promise to ship them at a future date, the seller can respond in either manner because the buyer did not adequately specify how the contract should be accepted.

Before modern statutes governing commercial transactions were adopted, the failure of a buyer to specify the manner of acceptance had an unfortunate result for the buyer because the seller could ship the requested goods and argue that they conformed to the order and thus constituted an acceptance or, alternatively, that they were nonconforming goods and did not represent an acceptance of the contract at all. New statutes eliminated this so-called "unilateral trick" by providing that if a seller filled an order by shipping nonconforming goods, it would be considered both an acceptance of the offer and a breach of the resulting contract. If the breach were serious enough to impair the value of the entire contract, then the buyer might choose to avoid the contract or offset the amount of damages against the value of the contract. In any event, this change now prevents the seller from avoiding contractual liability by asserting that the shipment did not create a contract.

This is not to say that the shipment of nonconforming goods will always act as an acceptance. If I ship you a walnut table in response to your order for a cherry wood table and I promptly notify you that the walnut table is being sent as an accommodation, then there is no acceptance and no breach of the agreement. You can accept the walnut table or send it back without any liability. Accommodation shipments usually occur in situations where the seller has some basis for believing that the substituted goods will be acceptable to the buyer or where the goods originally ordered and those sent as an accommodation have few significant differences and the seller believes the buyer would be indifferent about the differences.

An acceptance must be unconditional and unequivocal. If the offeree proposes any new terms, they will be treated as a counter-offer that terminates the original offer and the offeree's power to accept the original offer. An acceptance coupled with a condition, such as the statement "I will accept your offer to sell me your sweater if you will lower the price by five dollars," is treated as a counter-offer instead of an acceptance because the statement is not unequivocal. The acceptance is conditioned on the offeror agreeing to lower the price of the sweater by five dollars. As a result, the original offer is terminated and a new offer is made by the offeree to buy the sweater for the reduced amount. In the same way, an indefinite promise to consider the offer further is not an acceptance or a counter-offer. However, an acceptance coupled with a request, such as the statement "I accept your offer to sell me your sweater but I would appreciate it if you would lower the price by five dollars," would create an enforceable contract. In this case, the acceptance is not expressly conditioned on the price of the sweater being lowered by five dollars. It is more like a plea for a change of terms after the acceptance has been given. Whether or not the acceptance is conditional (and, therefore, a counter-offer) is not always clear; the resolution of this question will often depend on the particular factual situation in which the acceptance was given.

In most states, the offeree's timely acceptance of an offer for the sale of goods is valid even if it contains new or different terms, unless the offer was expressly limited to its original terms. The additional terms are treated as offers to modify the contract and they must be agreed to by the offeror before they become part of the contract. If the offeror does not agree to these terms, then they cannot be enforced. In the case of two merchants dealing with one another, however, any additional terms proposed by the offeree will be included in the contract unless:

- they materially alter the contract
- the offeror has expressly rejected them
- or the original offer was expressly limited to its own terms.

If a pickle merchant offered to sell a barrel of pickles to a store to be shipped by freight train, the request by the store that the barrel be shipped by a more expensive form of transportation would be a material alteration of the original contract. As a result, the new term changing the form of shipment would not be included unless the merchant expressly agreed. The same result would occur if the merchant had rejected the store's request that the pickles be shipped differently or if the original offer restricted the manner of shipment to railroad.

Certain problems can arise when the acceptance of an offer is made by mail. In general, the acceptance of an offer is valid when the acceptance is mailed. Offers and rejections and revocations of offers are valid only upon receipt at the proper address. To be effective upon dispatch, an acceptance must be sent in the manner authorized by the offeror or, alternatively, in any reasonable manner. In short, if the offeror requests that the acceptance be by mail and not telegram, then the acceptance will be valid when it is dispatched only if it is sent by mail. If it is sent by telegram, the acceptance will become valid only upon receipt.

When the offeree sends both an acceptance and a rejection, there are special rules to determine whether a contract has been formed. If the offeree sends a rejection then reconsiders and sends an acceptance, a contract will be formed only if the acceptance overtakes the rejection. If the rejection is received first, the offer is terminated. However, the acceptance in this case may constitute a new offer, which the original offeror may accept or reject. If the offeree sends an acceptance and then a rejection, a valid contract will be formed when the acceptance is mailed unless the rejection arrives before the acceptance and the offeror relies on that rejection. Reliance may be shown if the offeror somehow changes position in response to the rejection by the offeree of the offer. For example, if I receive your rejection of my offer to buy your car and, before receiving your acceptance, I purchase another car in reliance on your rejection, I will have changed my position sufficiently so that your acceptance is no longer relevant.

Consideration

It is useful to think of consideration as the value or inducement that motivates two parties to enter into a contract. A promise is supported by consideration (and thus enforceable) if the promisor has received a benefit or the promisee has incurred a detriment in exchange for the promise of the other party. Because each party must give up something in order to secure the performance of the other party, a promise that is not supported by consideration cannot be enforced.

In deciding whether a contract is supported by consideration, it is often necessary to examine the agreement to see whether one party did something that it would not have otherwise done in reliance on the promise of the other party. If I promise to pay you fifty dollars to go to church next Sunday, you would be able to enforce the promise if you actually did go to church because you acted in reliance on my promise to pay you and suffered a legal detriment. Even though attending church might be just the thing to make you a better person and therefore beneficial to you, your promise to attend causes you to suffer a legal detriment. Therefore, I must pay you the money because you responded in the manner called for by my promise. This transaction is a bilateral contract in which my promise to pay you fifty dollars is given in exchange for your promise to go to church.

A promise to pay someone for some good deed they did in the past does not create a binding contract because the benefit was conferred unilaterally at an earlier point in time. It was not given in exchange for the promise to pay. There must be a bargained for exchange or there is no contract. If I promise to give you my trading stamp collection because you ran errands for me when you were a child, you would not be able to enforce my promise because you did not agree to run the errands in exchange for my promise. However, if I promise to give you my stamp collection if you promise to run some errands for me, then we have created an enforceable bilateral contract.

Like past deeds, a statement of the motivation behind a promise to confer a benefit on another party is not sufficient to create a binding contract because there is no bargained for exchange of promises. Instead, there is only a gratuitous promise, which is unenforceable. My promise to give you fifty dollars because you have blonde hair (even if it is not chemically enhanced) cannot be enforced; you did not incur a legal detriment in exchange for my promise. If I promise to pay you fifty dollars in exchange for your promise to dye your hair blonde, however, then your reliance on my promise will cause you to incur a legal detriment and you will be able to collect the money from me.

The consideration that supports a contract must have some legal value. The courts are generally reluctant to interfere with how parties structure their contract. They will not inquire as to whether the consideration given is economically sufficient unless it appears that the agreement was a sham. If there is a vast discrepancy between the value of the consideration exchanged by the parties, it may suggest that the contract was fraudulent or that one of the parties was coerced or subject to the undue influence of the other party.

The problem of inadequate consideration arises in unconscionable contracts, which exist when the terms are extremely one-sided. The courts are especially alert to consumer contracts made by poor and illiterate buyers where the seller possesses overwhelming bargaining power and where there is an absence of alternative suppliers. If I am the only appliance dealer in a remote geographical area and I agree to sell a refrigerator to an illiterate buyer (who signs a contract with a clause allowing me to repossess it even if the final monthly payment is one day late), this contract will probably be declared unconscionable because the terms and conditions are so one-sided as to be considered fundamentally unfair. If a contract is found to be unconscionable, the court may void the entire contract or strike out the offensive clause or even interpret the offensive clause in such a manner so that it is no longer unconscionable. Because courts are reluctant to interfere with terms agreed upon by the parties to a contract, however, the complaint that a contract is unconscionable will succeed only when the discrepancies in bargaining power between the two parties are extreme.

In contracts where a much greater benefit is given in exchange for the payment of a small sum of money, such as one dollar, the contract will be upheld if the money was actually paid. The small sum is called nominal consideration. If the recited sum is not paid, however, then the one dollar is called sham consideration and the contract is not enforceable. Unlike the unconscionable contract where the courts try to assess the sufficiency of the consideration exchanged, the contract secured by nominal consideration will not normally be struck down by the courts because of their reluctance to examine the adequacy of the consideration given. Adequacy must be distinguished from sufficiency. A contract will be upheld so long as the consideration given has some value and there is no suggestion that the contract is unconscionable. Nominal consideration is often used to cast in contractual terms the conveyance of a gift: "In consideration of the sum of one dollar, I promise to convey my land to my son." Of course, the context in which the contract having nominal consideration is made will often determine whether there is a problem of unconscionability.

Nominal consideration must induce the promise by the other party, but it does not have to be the only inducement. I might desire to sell my house to my daughter at a price far below its market value because of the love and affection I feel for her. Obviously our personal relationship and not the nominal sum paid by my daughter for the house would be the primary inducement for my promise to sell the house to her for a nominal sum. As with other contracts, however, the nominal consideration must be given in exchange for the promise to sell the house.

A court may examine the adequacy of nominal consideration when it is used to disguise a gift as a contractual transaction. In such cases, the nominal consideration is not given in exchange for the property because the conveyance of the property is not induced at all by the recited sum. If I gave my son a car and then, almost as an afterthought, drew up a contract in which the recited consideration was to be paid to me in exchange for the car, there would be no bargained for exchange and this contract would not be binding. Another situation in which the courts look at the adequacy of the consideration is where there is an obviously uneven exchange of the same type of goods. If I promise to give you ten dollars of copper in exchange for your promise to give me five dollars of copper (perhaps because I never mastered the "new math"), then a court would probably ask whether there was adequate consideration for my promise.

One advantage of a written contract is that it specifies the rights and duties of each party and thus restricts the ability of any party to avoid its contractual responsibilities. If a party to a contract insists on maintaining an absolute and unconditional right to decide whether to perform, the contract is illusory. There must be some sort of restriction on a party's freedom of action or the contract will be unenforceable. One example of an illusory contract is my promise to pay you one hundred dollars if I feel like paying you in exchange for your promise to paint my tool shed. This is not the same as saying that I will pay you one hundred dollars for painting the tool shed only if the job is acceptable to me, because I am obligated to exercise my good faith judgment as to what constitutes a satisfactory paint job. If I am an extremely unreasonable person who believes that a good paint job must have at least six hundred coats of paint, my refusal to find the job acceptable will not prevent a court from enforcing the contract if it concludes that a reasonable person in this situation would have found the job to be satisfactory.

Closely related to illusory contracts are voidable contracts—legally binding agreements that may be disaffirmed by certain persons such as minors whom the courts wish to protect from their own imprudence. The power of a minor to avoid legal obligations is not unlimited because a minor cannot disaffirm a contract for necessities such as food and shelter. Voidable contracts appear to be similar to illusory contracts. However, there is consideration in a voidable contract because an affirmative act is required for the minor to void the contract. This requirement acts as a restriction on a minor's freedom of action, however minute, which prevents the voidable contract from being regarded as illusory.

A contract in which the performance of one party is not due until the occurrence of a specified condition is legally enforceable. If I promise to buy your sailboat only if my favorite hockey team wins the championship, I will be obligated to buy the sailboat once the stated condition has occurred. This statement is true even if the occurrence or nonoccurrence of the condition is totally within my control. If I promise to give you my old car if I buy a new car this year, you can enforce my promise when the stated condition occurs because the purchase will make my duty to perform absolute. The fact that I have sole discretion in choosing whether to purchase a new car this year or wait until next year is irrelevant.

An insurance policy is a sort of conditional contract because the benefits are paid only after the occurrence of an event that may or may not take place within the life of the policy. Insurance policies are known as aleatory contracts because they are triggered by the occurrence of an uncertain event such as the death of the insured. The consideration supporting the insurance policy is the promise by the insurer to pay the policy if and when the triggering event does occur. The theft insurance policy that I take out on my gold watch will not be paid until the condition or contingent event specified in the policy—the theft of the watch—occurs.

A contract where one party promises to use its best efforts is supported by consideration because an affirmative promise has been made. This promise obligates that party to make a good faith attempt to perform the promise. If I promise to act as the exclusive selling agent for a tennis ball manufacturer, the fact that the manufacturer is entrusting me with the sole responsibility for selling the products will obligate me to use my best efforts. Similarly, a requirements contract or option contract is supported by consideration because of the detriment incurred by the buyer or seller agreeing not to buy from or sell to another party. If I agree to sell all the baby carriages I can make to you, I have incurred a detriment and given consideration because I have given up my right to sell my baby carriages to another buyer. You have also incurred a detriment and given consideration because of your agreement to buy all the baby carriages I can produce. As a result, you must buy my entire stock before you are free to go to another manufacturer for any additional requirements you may have to satisfy.

Because a detriment can provide the necessary consideration to support a contract, there are a number of situations in which an agreement will be enforced solely because a loss or detriment is incurred by a party in exchange for a promise. An agreement by a creditor not to sue a debtor to collect an overdue debt will be sufficient consideration for a new promise by the debtor. If the creditor's claim is invalid—perhaps because the relevant statute of limitations (the time allowed by law to file a lawsuit for that claim) has expired—the agreement by the creditor not to sue may still be adequate consideration if the creditor reasonably believes that the claim is valid and well-founded. Where the detriment is not incurred in exchange for a promise, however, there can be no consideration to support a contract. One example occurs when a police officer captures a bank robber and tries to collect the reward offered by the robbed bank. Because the detriment (the duty to capture the bank robber) was within the police officer's pre-existing duties, no additional detriment was incurred in exchange for the bank's promise to pay. As a result, the officer would not be able to claim the reward.

There are situations when a promise given gratuitously by the promisor will be enforceable even though it is not given in exchange for consideration. Such a promise will be enforced if it causes the promisee to rely justifiably on it to the promisee's detriment. The doctrine of promissory estoppel is often used by the courts in situations where it would be unjust not to enforce the gratuitous promise. It is used to prevent the promisor from denying any responsibility for the promises that he makes (which cause the promisee to rely justifiably on that promise) on the grounds that the promisee gave no consideration. Unlike consideration, which is given in exchange for a promise, promissory estoppel is a device, which is applied after the gratuitous promise has induced the promisee's reliance, so as to avoid an unfair result. If I verbally promise to bequeath my polecat farm to you in my will and you rely on that promise by moving onto the land and spending a great deal of time and effort repairing the house and clearing the fields of stumps and rocks and installing air fresheners, the doctrine of promissory estoppel will apply and I will be forced to convey the land. Because you relied on my promise and expended so much labor improving the land, it would be unjust if I then turned around and said that you did not give any consideration in exchange for my promise. The work you did was valuable and would not have been done had I not made the promise.

Promissory estoppel may also be applied by the courts to enforce charitable pledges, especially in situations where the pledge causes the charity to undertake some activity or make some purchase that it would not have otherwise made. If a wealthy donor pledges one million dollars to endow a chair at a university, and the university, in reliance on that promise, hires a world-renowned scholar of gastrointestinal afflictions of songbirds to occupy that chair, the donor will be unable to assert that the promise was unenforceable. The donor's promise is binding because the university reasonably relied on it. If the donor were allowed to prevail, the university could be sued by the scholar for breach of the employment contract. To avoid this unfair result, the donor—whose promise caused the problem—will be forced to make good on the pledge.

Another common situation where the doctrine of promissory estoppel appears is in contract bidding. Most contractors who desire to bid on a building, for example, will seek bids from subcontractors to handle specific jobs within the building, such as electrical wiring or plumbing. The contractor will then take the low bid for each of the specific jobs and use those bids to calculate the bid on the building itself. To avoid the chaos that would result from allowing subcontractors to change their minds and withdraw their bids at will, the courts have used the concept of promissory estoppel to freeze the bids of the subcontractors when the contractor has relied on them in calculating the overall bid. It would be very difficult to build anything if a contractor could not rely on the bids of subcontractors for any significant length of time. As with the charitable pledge, the contractor gives no consideration in return for an irrevocable bid by the subcontractor. Moreover, the contractor is not legally bound unless and until the bid on the building itself is accepted. Whether it is fair to hold subcontractors liable to the contractor before the contractor's own bid has been accepted is debatable, but the courts are clearly willing to use the doctrine of promissory estoppel to bind the subcontractor bids and thus promote an orderly bidding process.

CHAPTER 2

The Formation of a Contract

Custom, that unwritten
law, by which the people
keep even kings in awe.

— Charles Davenant

2

The Statute of Frauds

We often make oral agreements with others in our daily lives because we feel that the subject matter is too trivial to justify putting the terms of our agreement into writing. I might offer you $5 to pick up a package for me today, but because our agreement is very straightforward and the duties clear—that I will give you $5 in exchange for your promise to pick up my package—we will probably not bother to put it in writing. Each of us makes many such oral agreements in the course of our daily routine in which we specify the duties of each party to the extent necessary to carry out the objective of the agreement. However, most of these agreements involve matters of such minor importance that we could not possibly justify the time needed to spell out in writing the responsibilities of each party. My promise to pick up and pay for a sandwich for you today in exchange for your promise to do the same for me tomorrow is an agreement that we do not feel is worth putting into writing because we are not dealing with a large amount of money. Moreover, we probably trust each other to some extent and do not anticipate—based on our past dealings—that we will need to go to court to enforce our agreement.

The point of this discussion is to show that it is simply not practical that all of our daily affairs be formally organized in written contracts. Moreover, it is not necessary to do so because many oral contracts are legally enforceable. The reason that we require written evidence (such as a bill of sale) in certain types of transactions is that we want the parties to consider seriously the terms of their agreement. We also want to have some physical evidence that could help resolve a disagreement between the parties as to their respective duties. The Statute of Frauds is a legal doctrine that requires that certain types of transactions be in writing or they will not be enforced by a court. Although there are many cases involving the Statute of Frauds in which the ignorance of one or both parties about the law has led to an unfair result, the courts have generally upheld its applicability in the situations outlined below.

A writing is always required when two parties agree to the sale of land or when one party agrees to lease land to another for more than one year. If the lease is for less than one year, an oral lease will be enforceable unless the state has enacted some law to the contrary. In cases where one party seeks to enforce the written agreement against the other, the writing must be signed by the latter or the agreement may be unenforceable. The reason for this requirement is that we do not want one party with an unsigned contract trying to force the other named party to comply with the terms of the agreement. Such situations would obviously lead to much fraudulent behavior if a signed consent was not needed.

In addition to the sale of land and a leasehold, there are other realty interests that must be created or transferred in a writing, including easements (the right of one landowner to make some beneficial use of the land of another, such as crossing over that land), mortgages, liens (a claim made against someone's property to secure payment of a debt), and licenses (a nonpossessory interest in land, such as the right to enter another's land and cut firewood). Because of the seriousness with which the courts view such transactions, they generally require that a party give written authorization to an agent acting on its behalf in such transactions. Consequently, if you wish to sell your house and ask a realtor to handle your property, most courts will not enforce that agreement unless it is in writing. Most realtors are acutely aware of this fact and will give you an agency agreement to sign before they lift a finger. This agreement will require you to pay a specified commission to the realtor (some fixed percentage of the total value of the sale) if the realtor finds a buyer that is ready, willing, and able to purchase your house.

Another type of contract that must be in writing is a prenuptial or antenuptial agreement. A prenuptial agreement is "an agreement entered into by two people who intend to marry each other which sets forth the rights of each person in the property of the other in the event of divorce or death."[1] Not surprisingly, prenuptial agreements are very popular with wealthy persons who wish to avoid the community property laws on the books in many states.

One of the most common prenuptial arrangements is for each party to reserve unto itself all assets that he or she owned at the time the marriage was entered into as well as any traceable proceeds (cash) from the sale of those assets. In so far as assets acquired during the marriage are concerned, the terms of these agreements vary markedly. Some call for an equal division of the wealth acquired during the marriage, while others exclude property acquired by gift or bequest (inheritance). Most agreements tend to split the marital property, but when there is only a single large asset such as a house, the court may order that it be sold and the proceeds divided. Regardless of the terms of the agreement, it must be in written form or it will not be enforced. The reason for this requirement is that when a marriage falls apart and the parties are seeking to influence the terms of the property settlement, the truthfulness of their testimony regarding oral promises made before the marriage is at best questionable.

The Statute of Frauds also applies to surety agreements in which one party agrees to be responsible for the debts of another. For example, I might wish to purchase a van Gogh painting for

---

[1] Steven H. Gifis, *Law Dictionary* (Woodbury, N.Y.: Barron's Educational Services, Inc., 1984), 354.

$30 million, but because I work as a welder at the local shipyard, the seller is not likely to take my offer seriously. If I can persuade a wealthy but perhaps small-brained acquaintance to answer for my debt, he will become my surety or the one who will make good on the debt if my finances are found wanting. To be covered by the Statute of Frauds, my acquaintance must not in some way be directly liable for the debt as would be the case if he and I had agreed to purchase the painting jointly. No writing would be required if we were buying the painting together, even though he had agreed to be the surety, because the transaction would benefit each of us equally. Such a situation would exist if I had promised to convey the painting to him in exchange for his having agreed to be a surety. Where the main purpose of the surety agreement is to benefit the surety, there is no need for a writing.

The Statute of Frauds also requires that sales of goods valued in excess of $500 be in writing to be enforceable. The word "goods" refers to tangible property such as a car, a chair, or even a fire hydrant, and not intangible services. By services, we mean the labor a plumber expends to fix a sink or the lessons we purchase from a piano teacher. When services are involved, a writing is not required, even though either the value of the services performed or the value of the goods provided with the services is greater than $500. This situation holds true only so long as obtaining the services is the primary purpose of the transaction, and the goods or materials are an incidental feature. In other words, if I hire a bricklayer to build a new planter in front of my house, I am hiring the bricklayer for her services. To perform the job, she will have to obtain a certain quantity of bricks and cement that may exceed $500 in value. Even though $500 in materials may be involved, I am primarily interested in securing the bricklayer's services, so the Statute of Frauds is not applicable. Of course, one way to determine whether services or goods predominate in a contract is to see whether the labor or materials is greater in value.

Unlike the sale of services, contracts for the sale of intangible property (not goods) such as stocks, bonds, patents, trademarks, and copyrights must be in writing if the value of the property is in excess of $5,000. Like a contract for the sale of real estate, the contract for the sale of intangible property must describe the property in sufficient detail, specify a definite price, and include the signature of the party against whom the contract is to be enforced.

Several other features of the Statute of Frauds must be noted to give a clearer understanding of its scope. It does not apply, for example, to goods that are specially manufactured for a buyer, because the uniqueness of these goods prevents them from being resold thereby enabling the manufacturer to recover its costs. Unique goods have little or no resale value. If I hire a flag company to make fifty flags with my profile set out in grey on a field of pink, it is unlikely that the flag company will be able to sell these flags to someone else if I try to back out of the deal. Although such a flag may display considerable artistic flash, it is not likely that many people are going to purchase one to fly at home or over the local schoolhouse. There is no other market for the flags, so the seller will suffer a total loss on the deal if I do not keep my end of the bargain. To avoid situations of this sort, the courts do not require contracts for specially manufactured goods to be in writing if the manufacturer has substantially begun to perform or has incurred substantial costs in setting up the manufacturing process before the buyer gives notice that he does not intend to fulfill the contract. Of course, if I tell the flag company not to make the flags before it has incurred any costs or manufactured any products, then I will not be held responsible if it chooses to ignore me. A basic requirement of contract law is that the parties to a breached contract must take whatever reasonable actions are necessary to mitigate or minimize the damages. In the case of the flag company, it could mitigate the damages by stopping the manufacture of my flags once it received notice that I did not intend to go through with the purchase.

There are a number of situations in which a transaction can be taken out of the Statute of Frauds so that the absence of a writing does not bar its enforcement. One such example is when two merchants come to an agreement orally (during a telephone call) and one sends a confirmation letter to the other reciting the terms of their oral agreement. The confirmation letter must be sent within a reasonable time of the conversation. As long as the party receiving the letter does not object to its contents within ten days, the letter will satisfy the writing requirement of the Statute of Frauds.

If a party in a lawsuit admits during pleadings or testimony that a contract of sale was made, then the Statute of Frauds does not apply even though no written record exists. Such a situation might occur if I was a defendant in a breach of contract case and was being cross-examined by a clever lawyer while on the witness stand. At the appropriate time, I might choose to make a clean breast of things and admit that I did agree to purchase a high-powered rifle from the plaintiff, a reputable black market arms dealer. As a result, our oral agreement would no longer be rendered unenforceable by the Statute of Frauds since I would have admitted in court that such a contract exists. Whether the agreement might be voided on the grounds that it is promoting an illegal objective would depend on the gun laws of that particular state.

The partial performance of an oral contract takes that contract out of the Statute of Frauds to the extent that performance is given or payment is made. I might make an oral agreement with a confectionary company to buy three truckloads of cotton candy for $1,000 each because I have a hankering for sugar. If the first truck dumps its load on my lawn and I give the driver a check for $1,000 signifying my acceptance of the same, my oral agreement with the confectionary company is taken out of the Statute of Frauds so far as that part of the contract is concerned. I am under no obligation to take the other two deliveries because they are not covered by a written agreement. However, if the same series of events repeats itself twice more and I tender payment for two more deliveries of cotton candy, then the entire contract will satisfy the Statute of Frauds. My front yard might be covered by three feet of sticky melted candy, but I cannot point to the Statute of Frauds and say that I did not have an enforceable contract with the confectionary company, because we have both fulfilled our parts of the oral agreement.

The Statute of Frauds must also be considered when two parties make an agreement that, by its terms, cannot be performed within a year. If I lease an Edsel for five years, then my lease must be in writing to be enforceable, because it cannot be fully performed in a single year. If I decide to lease the Edsel for only six months, then the contract can be fully performed within one year. The six-month lease does not have to be in writing, although it is unlikely that many rental agencies would give me a car in exchange for my solemn oath to bring it back intact in half a year. Most companies use written contracts in all of their transactions with consumers regardless of the value of the goods sold or leased or the duration of the contract, because they want to have a file that will document their side of the story should they have to go to court to recover possession of the property. A written agreement also protects the consumer from abusive behavior by the company by setting forth each party's responsibilities (and noting any down payment made by the buyer). Thus it is in the customer's interest to have the terms of the agreement in writing.

The Statute of Frauds does not apply to contracts in which the time needed for performance is uncertain. If I promise to go work as a butler for my great

Aunt Agatha (who has no heirs, a bad heart and is worth $50 million) for the rest of her life because I am genuinely fond of her company and want to make her remaining years as comfortable as possible (perhaps by encouraging her to take up marathon running), my contract with her does not have to be in writing to be enforceable because Aunt Agatha might die before a year has passed (but hopefully not before she has had a chance to revise her will). If we agree that I shall buttle for her so long as she is satisfied with my services, then our contract does not have to be in writing, because she may sack me within a year for some atrocity such as stepping on her cat. If I agree to be her butler for a definite time period in excess of one year, however, the contract must be in writing, even though Aunt Agatha might leave this world before a year has passed.

When we talk about a contract being put into writing, the question arises as to what this writing must contain to satisfy the Statute of Frauds. We have already touched upon some of the items that must be included in a writing; perhaps the most important is a genuine signature by the party against whom we are seeking to enforce the contract. As noted above, this requirement exists primarily to reduce the possibility of fraud, but it is not necessary that we have a complete signature for the document to be valid. Many courts have upheld cases in which a party signed just initials or even some distinctive marking that could be attributed only to that party. If my name is Bartholomew Nebuchadezzar and I have always signed my papers with a B overlaid with an N to save time, that sort of signature will be perfectly valid. If I am a member of a unique religious sect called the "Bleeders" and one of my basic beliefs is that I can only sign legally binding documents with three drops of my blood, my drippings probably will not be considered a valid signature, because there is little to distinguish one bloodstain from another when viewed with the naked eye. The fact that certain genetic tests might be able to trace my blood directly to me is not relevant, because we are interested in promoting contractual agreements between individuals. We do not want to have to call in a geneticist every time someone signs a credit card slip at the department store.

In addition to a valid signature, a writing must also identify the parties. The identification must be specific enough so that no obvious ambiguities exist. Perhaps there are several other persons named Bartholomew Nebuchadezzar who live in my town. This potential confusion can be resolved by including my home address in the contract. Credit card slips usually have both an address and an account number to clarify further the identity of the buyer. This situation is not always an unqualified blessing, as people receiving their Christmas credit card statements will admit, but it does reduce the likelihood that the wrong person will be billed.

The subject matter of the contract must also be spelled out in the contract. If I sign a contract to purchase one ton of manure because I want to spread it over my yard to enrich the soil and keep the neighborhood children away, I can wave my copy of the contract in the face of the delivery driver when he insists on dumping *five* tons of manure on my lawn. If the driver is a persistent fellow who waits until I go to work the next day before depositing his cargo, my copy of the contract will serve as evidence that I purchased only one ton of manure in the event that I have to sue the manure company to force them to remove the extra four tons from my lawn. If I am fortunate, the matter will not have to go to court, since the quantity of my purchase is clearly specified. In such cut and dried circumstances, a reputable manure company would generally remove the excess voluntarily to avoid incurring court costs and consumer wrath.

Finally, a writing must contain the essential terms and conditions of the agreement. To return to my manure purchase, one condition of the contract might be that the manure be delivered at my home on January 15, because I am scheduled to leave town one week later and want to have seven days to spread the manure around the flower beds. Another condition of the contract might be that the manure be delivered in bright yellow plastic bags instead of the traditional burlap sacks generally preferred by professionals in the excrement business.

This situation highlights the distinction that must be made between relevant and irrelevant terms and conditions. The date of delivery is very relevant because, if the manure does not arrive at my house until seven days after the date called for in the agreement, I might be greatly inconvenienced by having to spread it around on the day of my trip. If it arrives after I have left town, then the pile of manure will sit on the lawn until I return, beckoning whatever vermin and insects are attracted to such things. I might return to find my yard infested with undesirable creatures and my house permeated by the smell of the barnyard. Consequently, a late delivery may be a material violation of this contract unless I have agreed beforehand that the delivery date can be changed. The fact that the delivery driver brings the manure to me in burlap sacks is also a violation of the contract, but it is probably irrelevant (even though it may offend my sense of aesthetics) because the color of the sacks has nothing to do with the essential subject matter of the agreement. The point of this digression is that all of the material terms and conditions of the agreement must be spelled out to avoid unpleasant surprises.

In certain situations, the requirement of a writing may be excused because events will have transpired so as to make the application of the Statute of Frauds counterproductive or absurd. If my Aunt Agatha conveys to me a piece of property known as Barrymore Estate based on my oral promise to pay its selling price, the fact that she has already deeded the property to me in reliance on my promise to pay for it takes this transaction out of the Statute of Frauds. Even though this is a transaction involving real estate, the courts want to protect Aunt Agatha's expectation that she will be paid and also force me to live up to my promise to pay her for the property. Aunt Agatha has already fully performed her part of the agreement, so it would be unjust to hold that the agreement is unenforceable because it is not in writing.

If I pay my Aunt Agatha for Barrymore Estate before she conveys it, the oral contract is not enforceable, because I may sue to have my funds returned should she refuse to go ahead with the deal. However, if I pay Aunt Agatha and then take possession of Barrymore Estate by moving into its charming neo-Gothic mansion, which reminds the neighbors of an exotic prison, and making significant improvements to the property (such as deepening the moat, refurbishing the dungeon, and perhaps getting new cannons for the turrents) then most courts will uphold the oral sales agreement. Because I have fulfilled my obligations and added significant value to the property by my improvements, the courts want to protect my expectation interest. They will order Aunt Agatha to go ahead with the transaction.

The Statute of Frauds defense may also be waived if it is not raised in a reasonable time. We discussed above the use of a letter of confirmation in which the letter served as a written memorandum of the oral agreement. If I am a mongoose pelt merchant and I send a letter of confirmation to a prestigious Fifth Avenue furrier codifying a previous oral agreement, the failure of the furrier to object to the terms of the letter of confirmation within the allotted time (usually ten days) will waive the Statute of Frauds defense. In other words, if the furrier waits too long before complaining that the letter does not accurately describe the terms of our original agreement, she will be unable to assert that the Statute of Frauds should bar the enforcement of the contract.

The Statute of Frauds may also be excused if a court finds that a party justifiably relied to its detriment on the other party's promise not to raise the Statute of Frauds defense to defeat an oral agreement. If I orally agree to sell a thousand mongoose pelts to the Fifth Avenue furrier for $5,000 on February 1 and then turn down an offer made the following week by a Park Avenue furrier to purchase these very same pelts (which I would otherwise have accepted as there are very few companies willing to purchase mongoose pelts), the Fifth Avenue furrier will be estopped (prevented) from wriggling out of the deal, even though it was an oral agreement valued above $500. The court will determine whether my reliance on the Fifth Avenue furrier's promise not to raise the Statute of Frauds defense was reasonable. If the court decides that I did reasonably rely on the Fifth Avenue furrier's statements, then the court will examine whether I suffered a loss as a result. Since I turned down another offer by the Park Avenue furrier to purchase those very same pelts, I certainly suffered a lost sale that I could have made had I not made the earlier agreement with the other furrier. Consequently, it is unlikely that the Fifth Avenue furrier will be able to assert successfully that the Statute of Frauds should bar enforcement of our contract.

Chapter 2

Parol Evidence Rule

Despite its name, the Parol Evidence Rule is actually a rule of contract law, not evidence. In short, it is a rule of construction that is used to exclude evidence of prior or contemporaneous negotiations that are not reflected in an unambiguous written agreement when that document is intended to be the final expression of those negotiations. If I am negotiating with my Aunt Agatha to purchase her beloved Barrymore Estate, we will likely engage in many tactical maneuvers during our discussions. I may ask my Aunt Agatha to include the catapult on the roof in the deal and she may refuse, arguing that it is a valuable antique that she wants to keep for herself. Twenty minutes later she might have a change of heart and offer to give me the catapult for taking the house off her hands. If the written contract spelling out the terms of our agreement says that the catapult is to be included in the bill of sale, then the parol evidence rule will prevent my Aunt Agatha from introducing any evidence that I mumbled something during our negotiations about donating the catapult to the Metropolitan Museum of Art. Although the Parol Evidence Rule appears at first glance to be expansive in its scope, the courts have tended to interpret it narrowly.

The Parol Evidence Rule comes into play only if it is clear that the contract is intended to be the final and complete expression of the agreement between the parties. An integration clause is often included at the end of an agreement; it typically states that the substance of the agreement is codified in the written document and that all other evidence at variance with the terms of the agreement should be excluded. The integration clause creates the presumption that the contract is complete and self-contained unless there is some overt evidence of fraud, such as a forged signature or additional terms not common to all copies of the contract. The Parol Evidence Rule, in fact, does not prevent one party from introducing evidence that the written agreement is not intended to be complete. To return to the sale of Barrymore Estate, if the language describing the property being sold is unclear whether its fine antiques such as the catapult are to be included with the house, and Aunt Agatha and I had agreed during our negotiations to go ahead with the sale and worry about what to do with the antiques later, then it would be proper for either of us to bring this matter up later as it was not resolved. Since we did not intend for the contract of sale to be final in this respect, the Parol Evidence Rule would not prevent either of us from raising this point.

The Parol Evidence Rule also would not prevent either of us from offering evidence relating to a collateral matter. A collateral matter is one that is not central to the main purpose of the contract (the sale of Barrymore Estate). A collateral issue might be whether I will continue to employ Otto Hertz, the enthusiastic but generally incompetent gardener (who has never been adept with an edger but can machete hedges with the best of them). Though Aunt Agatha might dearly want me to keep Otto on the payroll as a way of getting out of her own employment commitment to him, this is arguably a collateral issue, because whether Aunt Agatha or I agree to employ Otto is not really central to the sale of Barrymore Estate. Because any employment agreement involving Otto would likely be in a separate document and the money for his salary would probably be paid pursuant to that agreement, it is a collateral matter. The Parol Evidence rule would not prevent either Aunt Agatha or I from bringing up who will be Otto's future employer, because that issue is not central to the property sale.

Although the Parol Evidence Rule bars evidence that contradicts or modifies the terms of an integrated (complete) agreement, it does not exclude evidence that is used to resolve an ambiguity or to show that there was some defect in the formation of the agreement. If the Barrymore Estate agreement has a clause stating that the property is located at "321 Honeysuckle Road" when it is actually located at 123 Honeysuckle Road, it would be absurd for the Parol Evidence Rule to prevent me from pointing out that the address is incorrect. Similarly, if during the course of negotiations I ply my Aunt Agatha with many glasses of her favorite brandy so that she becomes a little fuzzy-headed and signs an agreement conveying her property to me for a dollar (something she would normally not have done), then Aunt Agatha is free to point out that she was not quite herself when she signed the agreement. Since Aunt Agatha was not totally lucid at the time, there was a defect in the formation of the agreement and the Parol Evidence Rule will not bar this evidence. In desperation, I might say that the sum of one dollar was a nominal amount intended to cover an outright gift of Barrymore Estate to me, but that argument would not be very helpful if the court believed Aunt Agatha.

While the Parol Evidence Rule excludes evidence of prior or contemporaneous negotiations up until the signing of the contract, it does not exclude evidence about negotiations following the signing of the contract, even though this evidence may deal with the same subject matter. It is true that this evidence must be relevant to the transaction, but the courts tend to construe that requirement liberally. There is no mechanical formula for deciding whether a fact is relevant, but a good test is whether it contributes in some manner to resolving the question in dispute. If I agree to pay Aunt Agatha in cash for Barrymore Estate at the time of closing, but we later agree that I will pay her one-fifth of the purchase price for each of the next five years, then evidence of this subsequent negotiation is clearly relevant to the contract. On the other hand, if Aunt Agatha and I agree that I will plant posies next year in the flower bed even though I would have preferred to build a swimming pool there, these negotiations would probably be excluded as irrelevant, because they are not directly related to the sale of Barrymore Estate. A different outcome might result if Aunt Agatha could convince the court that the only reason she sold me Barrymore Estate was that I promised to maintain a bed of posies in honor of her recently-departed tabby cat. In such a situation, this information might appear to be more relevant.

Chapter 2

Illegal Contracts

The Parol Evidence Rule is not the only thing that we must consider when we are trying to draft a legally binding contract. No matter how skillful the drafter, a contract having a illegal objective will not be enforced by the courts. If I sign an agreement to purchase an elephant gun from a gun dealer in a jurisdiction where the sale or possession of firearms is illegal, then neither of us will be able to sue the other for the nonperformance of the contract. Though I may have wanted an elephant gun dearly since I was a young lad because I thought it would help me win friends and influence people, the court will ignore my heartfelt pleas that the gun dealer be forced to convey the weapon to me even though I am willing to part with a fistful of cash. Similarly, the gun dealer will not be able to take me to court and obtain a judgment ordering me to go through with the purchase. Such a contract is void on its face, which means that it is without legal effect. A void contract must be distinguished from a voidable one where the contract is given legal effect unless one or both of the parties decides to declare it void.

A contract need not be strictly illegal to be void. If the objective of the contract promotes some interest or result that is highly offensive to the public's morality or tastes, then it may be treated as null and void. If I contract with a carpenter to install a billboard on my front lawn displaying scantily-clad women in suggestive poses, a local group of concerned citizens might be very offended by my plans. In fact, they might go to a judge and convince her to issue an injunction, preventing the carpenter from starting work. Though my pleas about the artistic merit of my billboard might be sympathetically received, the judge will probably be reluctant to get on the bad side of the concerned citizens with a judiciary election around the corner. But the judge will try to assess whether my proposed billboard would offend the town's morality by hearing testimony from a number of local citizens as to whether they find the billboard to be vulgar, tasteless and utterly lacking in artistic value. This testimony will provide the judge with the information about the local attitudes towards my billboard that she needs to decide whether to tear up the contract.[2]

A slightly different sequence of events would follow if my fellow townspeople were earthy people who delighted in breaking as many of the Ten Commandments in a single day as they could and in building billboards on their own front lawns depicting profane scenes. Given my neighbors' rather limp sense of morality, it is unlikely that my comparatively modest billboard would elicit much protest. Nor does it appear likely that the validity of my contract would

[2] I am ignoring any First Amendment arguments ("freedom of speech") that might be put forth to defend anything of questionable literary or artistic value (such as the racy billboard) to show that some contracts can be so blatantly offensive to community tastes that they can be suppressed. For something to be considered obscene and thus outside the protection of the First Amendment, for example, the Supreme Court requires that it be patently offensive; it must also appeal to the prurient interest and lack serious literary, artistic, or scientific value.

be questioned. If some miracle occurred (the day after I signed the installation contract with the carpenter) and my neighbors suddenly began to straighten up and fly right, throwing their whiskey bottles away and dismantling their obscene billboards, then my proposed billboard might now be viewed as offensive to the community. Since we are not talking about a law being enacted against billboards but simply a complete change in community attitudes toward titillating billboards, the contract would be rendered void not because the objective is technically illegal, but because it is impossible to perform the contract without violently offending the public's newly-embraced sense of decency.

There are a number of transactions that the courts do not enforce, such as agreements to commit fraud, to impede the judicial process, to impair one's right to marry, to restrain competition unreasonably, or to commit a crime. To take the first situation, if you and I sign an agreement to sell some worthless stock certificates to my Uncle Harold and you get cold feet at the last moment and back out of the deal, I cannot take you to court to enforce our agreement. The courts would treat such an agreement as a nullity and refuse to enforce it because they do not want to encourage fraudulent transactions. Even if our transaction involves legitimate but speculative stock certificates that I merely want you to praise as though they were blue-chip stocks, any such actions would still constitute a misrepresentation of fact and our agreement would not be upheld.

A contract to impede the judicial process could take many forms. One example might occur if I were clocked for speeding and made an agreement with a friend that the friend would slip the judge some money so that he would look on my story more favorably. If my friend decided that there was something fishy about this transaction, I would not be able to sue her to enforce the agreement because our contract would not be given legal effect by any court. Similarly, any attempt on my part to induce another person to bribe a juror or a police officer would not be kindly regarded by the courts and would certainly not constitute a binding agreement.

If I offer to give my sister Matilda $10,000 if she will leave her husband (whom I have never liked and always considered to be of some lower species), our agreement would not be enforced, because the purpose of my offer is to destroy her marriage. The courts are very much in favor of marriage; they view it as a cornerstone of modern society and would not be kindly disposed to an enterprising fellow who encourages his sister to file for divorce. If anything, the courts have supported marriage more emphatically in recent years owing to the great increase in the number of divorces; they would probably view my actions even more harshly than in the past.

Agreements that unreasonably restrain competition between businesses or the employment opportunities of a former employee are not enforced because the courts want to promote competition in our society and encourage the free movement of people to jobs for which they are best suited. One of the most common situations occurs when one person buys out the business of another and asks the latter to sign an agreement promising not to compete with the purchased business for a certain amount of time within a specified geographical area.

I might have my heart set on opening a hardware shop, but I might want to avoid the time and aggravation of building a business from scratch. As a result, I might purchase an existing business such as the Hardware Emporium located in the center of my town. However, I do not want to pay a lot of money for the Hardware Emporium only to see its present owner, Mr. Sprocket, set up a new store a few blocks away and take all of the Emporium's existing customers. To protect myself, I might add a clause to the sales contract preventing Mr. Sprocket from competing with his former business. Because I know that Mr. Sprocket has a devoted clientele, I might include a term in the contract stating "Mr. Sprocket agrees that he will not open a competing business in the continental United States for the next 500 years." The beauty of this provision is that it would confine Mr. Sprocket to Alaska and Hawaii if he chose to open a new store in the United States. In addition, it would prevent the next fifteen generations of his descendants from opening a hardware store in the continental United States. These terms should be onerous enough to prevent any mass defections among my new customers.

The problem with this plan is that a court would find the terms of this noncompetition clause to be unconscionable and would refuse to enforce it. Alternatively, a court might tailor it more narrowly with respect to geography and duration by limiting its scope to the town limits and its duration to several years. The courts do not want to restrain Mr. Sprocket's ability to start a new hardware store any more than is absolutely necessary for me to establish my own business. However, the courts do realize that I am purchasing the goodwill of Mr. Sprocket's former business along with his customer list and the store's physical assets; the courts will permit a reasonable noncompetition agreement so that I can protect my investment.

The same reasoning underlies judicial attitudes toward employer-employee noncompetition agreements. If I hire workers for the Hardware Emporium and as a condition of the job require them to sign an agreement that they will not work for a competing store upon leaving my employment, a court would examine the scope of this restriction to determine whether it can be justified. I would probably have a difficult time arguing that my paint mixer, Felix Broosh, should be prevented from working for another hardware store because he might reveal his stirring technique or some other vital trade secret. As paints are mixed using predetermined quantities of various colors and very little in the way of independent judgment on the part of the employee is required, I would be hard-pressed to convince a court that the noncompetition clause should be upheld. A different result might ensue if my accounts executive Boswell Barron left my employment, because he would be familiar with my customer list and could do a great deal of damage to my business by sharing his knowledge with a competitor. In this case, I would have a legitimate reason for asserting that Boswell should not be permitted to work for a local competitor such as the Very Fine Hardware Shop; the argument that the noncompetition clause is simply a penalty for leaving my employment would hold less water here.

It is not surprising that an agreement to commit a crime would not be enforced. If I have always coveted my next-door neighbor's harp, but he has turned down my offer to purchase it because it is a family heirloom and not for sale, I might decide to hire myself a professional burglar to snatch the instrument. Even though "Sticky Fingers" Louie and I sign a binding contract stating that he will steal the harp and bring it to me in exchange for my payment to him of $1000, I would not be able to sue Louie if he tries to get out of the deal. The courts enforce contracts only when they have as their objective some legal and socially desirable goal. Very few courts would consider my effort to boost the income of a thief to be praiseworthy. I might be able to prove that I can play the harp better than my next-door neighbor or that his son cheats in school and does not deserve to inherit such a wonderful instrument, but the court will ignore my pleas because it does not want to encourage contracts to commit crimes.

If I sign an agreement having a perfectly legitimate purpose, such as the sale of spray paint, that contract will be upheld even though I might have a strong suspicion that the purchaser plans to use the spraypaint to deface some buildings. In this situation, my contract would only indirectly aid the accomplishment of an illegal act, so it would not be rendered unenforceable if I later sue the purchaser for passing a bad check. A different outcome might result if I sell some plutonium to a mentally unbalanced nuclear physicist, because plutonium is a highly regulated substance and its possession or sale by a private citizen is a crime. Unlike the sale involving spray paint (a product with a variety of legitimate as well as illegal uses), there are very few things one can do with plutonium other than construct an atomic bomb. As a result, I would not be able to argue that I sold the plutonium for a legitimate reason, such as the physicist's desire to add a sample to his rock collection. That type of argument would not impress most courts.

When a contract is procured by fraud, duress, or undue influence, then the contract may be voided by the party whose consent was wrongfully obtained. Although we have discussed fraudulent transactions already, we should emphasize that for a party to succeed on a claim that it has been defrauded, it must establish that it relied on a material misrepresentation of fact in deciding to go ahead with the agreement. If I have a fancy sports car that is precision-engineered except that its brakes give out at high speeds, my statement to a prospective buyer that the car is in tip-top condition would be fraudulent. Because my statement implies that the car has working brakes, it is a material misrepresentation of the condition of the car. However, the purchaser must also prove that she relied on my material misrepresentation. Otherwise she cannot claim that I have defrauded her. If my customer is a mechanical engineer who designs the brake systems of the very type of car that I am trying to sell, then she has the expertise to check out the brakes personally and cannot plausibly claim to have relied on my statement.

A different outcome might result if I made it impossible for this customer to check out the car so that she had no choice but to rely on my statement in deciding to go ahead with the purchase. For example, I might conveniently lose the car keys so that my customer could not take the car out for a drive and discover the otherwise undetectable flaw in the brakes. In such a situation, the purchaser would have to rely on my statements regarding the car's fitness, because she would have no other way to test it. As a result, she would be able to assert that she relied on my fraudulent statements although one would have to question the intelligence of anyone who would buy a used car without first taking it for a drive.

A slightly different situation would occur if I failed to volunteer some fact about the car such as its bad brakes or its leaky gas tank. In general, I am under no obligation to disclose these defects on my own; if I am asked about the fitness of the car, however, I must not make any material misstatements of fact. The only time that I would have to disclose these defects on my own would be if I stood in some sort of fiduciary relationship with the other party. If I was the attorney for Edward Cobbleston, a young man who had inherited $500 million when his parents' yacht was rammed by a wandering garbage scow, I would have an affirmative duty to disclose any material defects in the car if I tried to sell it to him. The rationale behind this requirement is that I am supposed to be looking out for Edward's legal interests and I cannot take advantage of my position as one of his trusted advisors to foist my car on him. I would have to disclose fully the condition of the car before completing the sale.

Duress and undue influence are two other areas in which a contract may be voided by an injured party. If I threaten my Aunt Agatha with some unspeakable crime (moving in next door to her is not enough; it must be some threat of physical harm) and that threat causes her to sign an agreement giving me a valuable gift or a large amount of money (something she would not have done absent this threat), then she is at liberty to void the contract, because my threat overcame her free will to dispose of her property as she pleases. Undue influence, by contrast, is usually found when a fiduciary or family relationship exists and one party takes advantage of the mental or physical infirmities of another. If I take care of my enfeebled Uncle Horace's daily affairs so that he is utterly dependent on me for everything from his meals to his mail, I could be accused of exercising undue influence if I convinced him to sign a contract in which he conveyed to me his valuable collection of black velvet paintings for a ridiculously low price. In such a situation, Uncle Horace would be able to void the contract by claiming that his dependence on me made him susceptible to being unduly influenced by my statements.

When talking about illegal contracts, we must point out that regardless of whether one or both or neither of the parties has performed its duties under the agreement, the courts will treat the contract as having no legal effect. In general, they will not intervene on behalf of one party who has fully performed even though the other party may have done absolutely nothing. If I offer a bookmaker $500 to lay bets on several horses in a state where such betting is illegal, the fact that the bookmaker pockets the money and fails to place the bets will not make any difference. The court will not order the bookmaker to return the money; it will simply void the agreement and leave us in our current situation. While I might be cheered if the bookmaker gets run down by a bus, I will not be able to use the legal system to recover my money. Of course, if we made this agreement in a state where horse betting was legal, then I would be able to sue the bookmaker for the recovery of my money.

There are some exceptions to this rather harsh judicial rule of refusing to enforce illegal agreements, such as when one party is misled as to the illegal nature of the contract and signs the agreement believing that it is legally binding. If I hire the well-known daredevil Mr. Frederico to go over Niagara Falls in a barrel to celebrate my birthday, the court might hold me to my promise to pay him for the stunt, even though Mr. Frederico broke the law by performing his part of the agreement. The court might find that Mr. Frederico (who speaks no English) justifiably relied on my statements that barreling over waterfalls is a national sport in this country and order me to pay the agreed amount to him despite my pleas that ours was an illegal transaction that should be voided by the courts.

When one party is mentally incompetent at the time the agreement is formed, the contract may be voided by a court. We want to encourage parties to make contracts of their own free will, but we do not want to have people taking advantage of persons who are not fully cognizant of the legal implications of their actions. Before a person has been declared incompetent by a court, any contract the person signs will be voidable; the incompetent party may disaffirm the contract and be relieved of his legal obligations. If a contract is signed after a person is declared mentally incompetent by a court, any subsequent agreements made by that party will be void and without legal effect. Although I might convince the completely dotty multimillionaire J. Frederick Reynolds to sell his house to me in exchange for some worthless Confederate money, he would be able to void the contract by establishing that he was playing with half a deck when we signed our contract. If we made our agreement after Reynolds had been declared incompetent by a court, then he would not actually have to disaffirm the contract; it would be void from its inception. If Reynolds regained his mental competency at some later date (possibly after a brain transplant), he would be permitted to ratify the contract we made although he would certainly not be required to do so.

A different situation would result if I had signed the contract with Reynolds but was unaware that he was missing a screw. In this case, Reynolds would not be able to declare the contract invalid unless he gave me my Confederate money back. If I was aware of his incompetency, however, then his declaration that the contract is void would shield him from having to give me the money back if he had already disposed of it. This rule discourages people from deliberately taking advantage of the mentally disadvantaged by imposing a penalty if the payment made or property conveyed has already been spent or otherwise transferred. These same rules apply to intoxicated persons. Any contract signed by an intoxicated person may be voided by that person after he sobers up. However, the person must be so drunk at the time the contract is signed that he cannot understand the legal effects of his actions. A single drink will not usually cause a person to become sufficiently intoxicated to be considered legally incompetent (unless the person is overly sensitive to alcohol). In any event, it is not a good idea to get your neighbor drunk and then persuade him sign over his camper for a dollar. Not only will he be able to rescind the contract when he recovers, but he may also be able to sue you for damages.

A minor is also deemed incapable of entering into a binding contract. Although we want people to keep their promises, the courts have carved out an exception for underaged persons, because they want to protect them from their less judicious decisions. Like persons who are mentally incompetent, minors may choose to disaffirm a contract, although this right is subject to certain exceptions. Some of these exceptions include contracts for necessities (food, clothing, and shelter), alimony, child support, bail bonds, insurance contracts, and military enlistments. Minors must also pay for the value of services performed before they actually disaffirm the contract. If a minor hires a plumber to bang on the basement pipes for an afternoon, she must pay the plumber for his services until the time she communicates her repudiation of the agreement to the plumber. For other types of contracts, however, a minor may choose to disaffirm the contract until she reaches the age of majority (usually eighteen years). After that age is reached, the contract will be legally binding. A person who enters into otherwise valid contracts while still a minor may also ratify these agreements upon reaching the age of majority.

One type of contract that the courts generally allow a minor to disaffirm are automobile purchases. This rule is grounded in public policy considerations. Young people often underestimate the expenses associated with buying and maintaining an automobile and overestimate their ability to meet these costs. To avoid the hardship that would result from holding adolescents to contracts they cannot afford, minors are usually able to disaffirm automobile purchase agreements. However, a minor does not need to return the car before asserting the defense of incapacity if it is no longer in her possession. This is the case even if the minor's actions have contributed to the automobile being lost, stolen, or damaged. As a result, most automobile dealers insist that an adult co-sign a purchase agreement and, in effect, agree to answer for the debt of the minor.

A contract does not have to consist of explicit promises to be binding; a contract may be inferred by a court if the conduct of the parties indicates that it was their intent to enter into a binding agreement. If I ask a plumber to come over and unclog the kitchen sink, he would usually expect to be paid for his work (unless he is an amateur plumber who goes around doing good deeds). My request that he come fix the sink would be treated as an offer that he can accept by showing up on my doorstep with his plunger in hand. Once he unclogs the sink, I would be legally bound to pay him for his labor even though I never explicitly promised to do so. Under the circumstances, most courts would find that an implied contract was created by our conduct.

CHAPTER 3

Mistakes, Conditions, and the Discharge of Legal Obligations

As to many opinions as there are men; each a law to himself.

— Terence

3

Once the rights and duties of the parties have been spelled out and a legally binding contract is formed, problems can arise regarding the way the subject matter of the contract is described. Questions may be raised as to what conditions must be satisfied before one party's performance is due or as to how particular contractual obligations are to be discharged. Equally important is what the rights and duties of each party will be if one of them is unable to fulfill its part of the agreement. A contract is not something set in stone; changes in circumstances often necessitate that the terms of an agreement be modified so as to save the agreement. Many people believe that a contract is the culmination of a legal relationship between two parties; it may be more appropriate to view the signed contract as only the first step in an ongoing partnership that will evolve over time depending on the type of agreement and the personalities and circumstances involved.

Chapter 3

Mistakes

A contract must accurately describe whatever item is being purchased or conveyed. Many contracts are often so poorly drafted that it is not clear at first glance what was purchased or sold. Even when the item is accurately described, however, events sometimes make it unclear as to whether the contract should be enforced. This situation may arise when a mutual mistake has been made by the parties regarding the exact nature of the goods that are being transferred.

If I am a weekend farmer who wants to buy a mare sired by a famous racing horse but does not want to spend the millions of dollars usually required for such a purchase, I might choose to purchase a sterile horse. Although this horse would offer no opportunity to make money from the sale of its progeny, its purchase would bring me some measure of notoriety and perhaps enable me to rub elbows with the local bluebloods. If I make an agreement with the owner to purchase the horse for $5,000, even though it would sell for several hundred times that amount if it were fertile, then it is clear from the low price that we both believe the horse to be sterile. We would both be very surprised to find that the mare was pregnant, and I would certainly be pleased that I had negotiated such a low price. Unfortunately, I would not be able to force the horse's owner to convey it to me, because we made a mutual mistake regarding the fertility of the horse when we initially set the terms of our agreement. We both thought the horse was sterile when it was actually pregnant. The courts would refuse to order the owner to go through with the deal—not because the horse is worth much more than the contract price but because a pregnant horse is completely different from the sterile horse that we both thought we were dealing with. In such a situation, there can be no mutual agreement and thus no enforceable contract.

Unlike a mutual mistake, a unilateral mistake occurs when only one party makes a mistake about the nature of the subject matter. A unilateral mistake in itself is not sufficient to enable the mistaken party to avoid the contract. A different situation arises, however, when one party makes a mistake about the subject matter of the contract and the other party is aware of the mistake but either does nothing to correct the erroneous impression or deliberately encourages it. If I mistakenly believed that the horse mentioned above was a descendant of the great racing champion Peg Leg and the owner deliberately encouraged my belief even though she knew that the horse's most famous ancestor was actually a children's zoo pony, then I would have grounds for avoiding the contract. This rule exists to encourage people to be accurate in the factual statements they make during contractual negotiations. If I was mistaken about some fact about this horse and the horse's owner did not know about my error, I would not be able to rescind the agreement, because it would be unfair to penalize the seller for something about which she was totally ignorant.

Because many people use agents to negotiate their contracts, the question arises as to who should bear responsibility for the agent's mistakes. In general, the party who hired the agent has to answer for any mistakes made by the agent. If I hire a German agent to handle my negotiations with the president of a major chemical company in Frankfurt about purchasing the North American distribution rights for a petroleum-based shampoo, and I specifically instruct my agent over the telephone to offer a maximum fee of $10,000 during his negotiations, I would still be held liable if my agent (whose English is not very good) misunderstood my instructions and offered the company a $100,000 fee. Although this very generous offer might surprise and delight the chemical company representatives (and cause my bankruptcy), I would be held liable for the entire amount, because I am responsible for making sure that my agent acts in accordance with my wishes.

A similar result occurs if there is some ambiguous term in the contract. The party that is responsible for this ambiguous term will have it construed against him or her. If my contract with an automobile dealer states that the sticker price includes air-conditioning but does not state which model of air-conditioner, the dealer would probably argue that the contract refers to the least expensive air-conditioner (a battery-powered hand-held fan), which is barely powerful enough to cool the front seat of a subcompact much less the "battlecruiser" station wagon that I have just purchased. Because it was the dealer's fault that the model of air-conditioner was not specified, the court would probably accept my argument that the air-conditioner should be a model powerful enough to cool the interior of the car and not just the dashboard. Consequently, the ambiguity regarding the model of air-conditioner included with the purchase of the car would be construed against the dealer.

If the ambiguity in the contract cannot be blamed on either party, or if we both interpret the ambiguity in the same way, then neither party should be penalized. If I sign a contract with a pet shop to purchase the first pelican that arrives in the store from the island kingdom of Kettlemettlegami and I expect that bird to be a rare ring-necked carnivorous pelican, the fact that the pet shop owner also interprets the word "pelican" to mean a ring-necked carnivorous pelican means that we have a mutual agreement. As a result, the contract is enforceable, because we both have the same interpretation of the ambiguity in mind. If, on the other hand, I had in mind a rare ring-necked carnivorous pelican and the pet shop owner believed that I wanted the more common blue-bottomed herbivorous pelican, then there would be no mutuality of agreement. Each of us would have a different interpretation of the word "pelican", so the contract would be unenforceable.

Conditions

A question often arises after a binding contract has been signed: When is the performance of one party actually due? Sometimes the language of the contract is very clear; it may require that one party perform on a certain date or before or after a certain event occurs or even at the same time that the other party performs its contractual dates. Because of the great variety of complex and detailed commercial transactions, the timing of each party's performance often depends on something more than just the passage of time. In other words, the language of the contract may require that some particular event occur before one party's performance becomes due, or it may condition the performance of one party on the simultaneous performance of the other party, or it may even excuse one party's duty to perform if some specified event occurs after that party's duty to perform becomes absolute. These events are known as conditions; they are events that will alter the legal obligations of the parties to a contract.

As suggested by the previous paragraph, there are three types of conditions that are essentially distinguished by their temporal features. A condition precedent is an event that must occur before a party's duty to perform becomes absolute. If I promise to give you my collection of returnable bottles only if the local javelin-catching team (the Midway Butterfingers) wins the national championship, then the condition that the team win the championship is a condition precedent to my duty to give the bottles to you. I am not obliged to do anything unless and until the Butterfingers hold their arms up in victory at the end of the championship tournament. Even if the Butterfingers are prevented from competing in the tournament by some unforeseen event, my duty to perform would not be triggered. Assuming that the Butterfingers do stand alone on the bloody corpse-laden field of victory when the championship medal is presented, then my duty to perform would be activated. My failure to convey the bottles to you at that time would make me liable for damages, because I did not perform my duties under our agreement.

Because the courts want to promote contractual agreements between individuals and minimize the uncertainty surrounding each party's rights and duties under the contract, they try to construe contracts so as to avoid conditions precedent. This is not to say that the courts will deliberately strike out a perfectly clear condition that must be satisfied before a party is obligated to perform its contractual obligations. However, if a condition precedent is vaguely worded, ambiguous, or unclear, the courts will tend to interpret it narrowly. As with other elements of any contract, a court will want to determine whether the condition precedent was actually contemplated by both parties—a variant of mutuality of agreement.

The next type of condition that one encounters are concurrent conditions where each party must simultaneously perform its obligations under the contract. A good example might be when the mailcarrier brings a delivery to my door, such as the twenty-volume *Great Works of Illiterate Authors,* and asks me to pay for the shipment since I requested that it be mailed C.O.D. (collect on delivery) when I placed my order. Since the mailcarrier gives the books to me at about the same time that I give her the money, we will essentially perform our contractual obligations simultaneously. This type of condition is most common in face-to-face transactions such as the one outlined above. We would be concerned with a condition precedent instead of a concurrent condition if I had mailed a check to the publisher directly to cover the cost of the books. Since the publisher would not mail the books to me until my check clears, the bank's approval of my draft might be considered a condition precedent for mailing the books.

A condition subsequent is an event the occurrence of which discharges what had previously been an absolute duty to perform. If I agree to appear in a soap commercial on the condition that it be filmed before the end of this calendar year, I would be discharged from my obligation if the year ends and the commercial has not been shot. My obligation to appear in the commercial was unconditional only for a limited amount of time. The passing of the present year was the condition subsequent that discharged me from my contractual responsibilities. Of course, my being released from my contractual duties has nothing to do with the passage of time itself; it was my specifying the amount of time that I would be available to fulfill this contract that was the critical action. In any event, I would be released from my unperformed contract when the clock strikes midnight on January 1. As with the other conditions, however, a condition subsequent is only legally effective if it is contemplated by both parties at the time the contract is signed.

When we talk about conditions, we must distinguish between express conditions and constructive conditions. An express condition must be complied with in all respects by one party in order to make the second party's duty to perform absolute or to discharge it from that duty (depending on whether the other party faces a condition precedent, a condition concurrent or a condition subsequent). Substantial compliance with an express condition is not enough to discharge the first party's duty to perform; even minor discrepancies in the first party's performance may render that party liable for damages. In addition, such incomplete performance excuses the other party from performing until the defects in the performance are cured.

If I agree to dress up as a pirate for a neighbor's birthday party in exchange for $50, my wearing a pirate costume is an express condition of that agreement, which must be fulfilled before my neighbor has to pay me the fee. If I have a change of heart en route to the costume store and later show up at my neighbor's house dressed as Cleopatra, then I would have breached the contract and obviously not have fulfilled the express condition of our agreement. Even though I might look quite the vampish Egyptian queen in my outfit, my neighbor's obligation to pay me the fee would be excused. He may even be able to sue me for money damages because of my imperfect compliance with the contract. Even if my neighbor finds me attractive when dressed in women's clothing, that would not alter the fact that I did not wear a pirate costume to the party as originally agreed.

A somewhat different situation occurs when one party's duty to perform is made expressly dependent on that party being satisfied with the performance of the other party. To return to our pirate example, if I had agreed to show up as a pirate even though my neighbor stated that payment of the fee was conditioned on his being satisfied with my pirate outfit, we would still have an enforceable contract, because my neighbor cannot unreasonably withhold his approval of my performance. We spoke in a previous chapter about illusory contracts in which one party really has no constraints as to whether it is required to perform or not perform its part of the agreement; the constraint in this situation is the requirement that my neighbor decide in good faith whether or not my pirate performance is satisfactory. If I show up in an authentic pirate's costume wearing a peg leg on my right knee instead of my left as requested by my neighbor, he would probably not be able to claim that I did not render a satisfactory performance, because the placement of the peg leg really does not affect the splendor and authenticity of my outfit. A court would probably rule in such a situation that my neighbor was being unreasonable and order him to pay me the fee. If I showed up wearing a moose outfit with a pirate hat balanced on the antlers and a sword in hand, then my neighbor would have some justification for claiming that I had not satisfactorily performed my part of the contract. Even though he might find the idea of a moose in a pirate's costume amusing, he would be able to claim that his reasonable expectation was not satisfied.

Unlike express conditions, constructive conditions are not specified in a contract but are implied by the courts to ensure that the parties are not unnecessarily penalized for the omission of a particular term, such as the form of payment for delivered goods. In short, constructive conditions are gap-fillers by which the courts can prevent one party from unfairly taking advantage of some unclear or omitted contractual language and thereby encourage the parties to deal with each other fairly. If I agree to purchase from Fred Fence (the owner of Fences, Fences & Fences) 2,000 yards of electrified fencing for my backyard, but Fred and I neglect to specify what form of payment must be made when the fencing is delivered, a court may fill the gap by saying that the payment can be made by check, even though Fred might prefer to be paid in cash. Because it is unlikely that I would have such a large amount of cash on hand, the court would probably say that it is unreasonable for Fred to demand cash on delivery unless he gives me enough time to get the cash together. After all, if a cash payment is so important to Fred, why did he not take the trouble to specify it in the contract?

When dealing with constructive conditions, we are not required to perform our contractual duties perfectly—unlike the situation we face when express conditions are involved. Because constructive conditions are inferred to promote fair dealings between the parties to a contract, the courts require only that substantial performance be tendered in order to make the other party's conditional duty to perform absolute. In the previous paragraph, we saw that my payment by check would generally be considered to be substantial performance of my contractual duties, so Fred Fence would not be able to refuse to deliver my electrified fencing. A different outcome would result if Fred had specified in the contract that payment was to be made only in cash at the time of delivery.

In that case, we would be dealing with an express condition that would have to be complied with completely.

How are we to define substantial performance? We might respond by saying that for a party's performance to be considered substantial, the unperformed part must be of little value relative to the performed part of the contract. In other words, the unperformed part of the contract must be insignificant enough so that it does not impair the value of the performance actually rendered by the party. In the electrified fence example, we would have to ask whether my payment by check represented a substantial performance of my duty to pay for the fencing. Assuming that the form of payment was unspecified, the court would likely hold that my payment by check instead of cash does not substantially impair the value of my performance (the payment itself) and at most would entitle Fred Fence to nominal damages (one dollar, for example). In such a situation, Fred would receive essentially the same benefit that he expected when he signed the contract.

Express conditions often appear in contracts in the form of "time is of the essence" clauses. This language means that the parties must perform their respective duties on a date provided in the contract; the failure by one or both parties to do so will constitute a major breach. These clauses often appear in realty and consumer goods contracts where the need for prompt and simultaneous performance by both parties is especially pronounced. If I sign a contract to buy some desert property fronting the eastern side of the San

Andreas fault (because I expect the strip of California to the west of the fault to one day slide into the Pacific Ocean and leave me with beachfront property), my sales contract will likely contain "time is of the essence" language that requires me to tender payment on the date specified in the contract. My failure to do so would constitute a material breach of the contract and entitle the seller to sue me for damages. Even though I might later decide to delay my payment after learning that I will have to wait a few hundred thousand years for western California to float off into the Pacific, I would be unable to wiggle out of my obligation to pay at the time of the closing. The "time is of the essence" language is relevant only to the time each party must perform; it has nothing to do with when I can make the most beneficial use of my newly acquired property.

Although conditions can often frustrate efforts by one party to secure the other party's performance, they are not immutable and may be excused when the needs of justice or fairness so require. Some of the most common situations in which conditions are excused occur when 1) one party has by word or deed waived the condition; 2) one party wrongfully interferes with the performance of the other party; or 3) one party by word or deed causes the other party to rely to its detriment on those words or deeds and thus fail to perform its contractual duties.

To take the first of these three situations, a waiver of a condition might be found when one party knowingly accepts an imperfect or defective performance by the other party even though the first party is entitled to reject that performance and refuse to perform its own contractual duties until the defective performance is cured. If I agree to purchase from a local art museum a bronze casting of Rodin's famous sculpture *The Thinker,* I would be entitled to reject the sculpture at the time of delivery if the figure was cast so that instead of his chin resting on one hand as is normally the case, the forefinger of that hand is stuffed up his nose. This defect in the sculpture would clearly constitute a defective performance by the museum of its duties under the contract, and I would be entitled to refuse to pay for the sculpture (thus suspending my performance). If I chose to accept the sculpture in its defective condition, I would waive my right to refuse to pay for the sculpture based on its defects. The act of payment would constitute a waiver of the condition that the sculpture be delivered in acceptable condition. My acceptance of the defective performance would not preclude me from suing the museum for any damages arising from the defective condition of the sculpture; it would only prevent me from being able to refuse to perform my part of the contract.

A condition will also be excused if one party behaves in such a manner as to prevent the other from performing a condition of the contract. If I promise Otto Hertz, my gardener, that I will pay him $1,000 to disassemble a thirty-foot statue of my late Uncle Harry (the long-suffering spouse of my Aunt Agatha), which she declined to remove when she sold me Barrymore Estate, we would have a binding agreement that would fall outside the pre-existing duty rule because such work is outside of Otto's traditional duty to putter around the grounds. Once Otto began to hack the statue apart with furious swings of his axe (thus demonstrating why he always received periodic increases in salary), I would not be able to avoid my obligation to pay him for the job by hiring a professional demolition crew to come in and blow up the statue. Otto would still be entitled to his $1,000, because it was only due to my hiring the crew that Otto was prevented from completing the job.

If I tell Otto that I am going to hire a work crew to remove the statue but that I will still pay him the agreed amount for his labors, it is likely that Otto will soon turn his attention to other things (such as how best to dig unsightly holes in the lawn) and forget the statue entirely. If he relies on my statement and abandons his efforts to decapitate the likeness of Uncle Harry, I should not be able to turn around and tell Otto that he will not be paid because he did not finish the job. My words caused Otto to stop hacking at the statue. It would be unfair to allow me to avoid paying Otto, because he justifiably relied on my promise to pay him before he abandoned the job. I am estopped from suspending my own performance even though I have released Otto from his obligation to remove the statue.

Extinguishing Contractual Duties

There are a number of ways in which a party may be released from its contractual duties even though it has not fully performed its part of the bargain. "When it is said that a contract is discharged, it is always meant that one or more of the legal relations of the parties have been terminated. The meaning that is most commonly intended is that the legal duty of one of the parties has been terminated. A party who is asserted to be under a legal duty by virtue of his contract may reply that the duty has been discharged by some factor that has occurred since the making of the contract."* The crux of this passage is that circumstances often occur which make it undesirable or unnecessary for one or both parties to perform their original agreement. Because it is always helpful to know when it is possible to wiggle out of one's obligations, we shall review several ways in which contractual responsibilities may be extinguished.

When both parties have signed an agreement in which they promise to perform particular duties, they may cancel their agreement if the contract has not been executed. When we talk about unexecuted or fully executory contracts, we are talking not about capital punishment but about the situation that exists when neither party has yet performed its contractual duties. In a situation where neither party has tendered performance, each party may agree to give up its right to the other party's performance in exchange for the other party doing the same. The release of each party by the other provides the necessary consideration for the mutual recision to be binding.

---

*Arthur Linton Corbin, *Contracts* (St. Paul, Minn.: West Publishing Company, 1952), §1228.

Chapter 3

We can better illustrate how mutual recision works if we suppose that I have signed an agreement with a vegetarian counselor in which I promise to pay him $1,000 in exchange for his teaching me how to resist meat and dairy products. If we meet at a local restaurant before beginning the program and I decide that this counselor is too extreme for my tastes (he insists that I give up nearly all of the basic food groups, including sugars and preservatives) and he decides that I am a lost cause (because I order a slab of pork to celebrate the beginning of my new health program), then we could mutually rescind our contractual obligations; I have not paid him and he has not begun giving me lessons in nutrition. We might also rescind our agreement to the extent of our remaining unperformed obligations if I had paid him $50 and he had given me the first lesson in his program.

If I completely perform my obligations under the contract (by paying the fee) and my vegetarian advisor has not done anything when we decide to terminate our agreement, we cannot mutually rescind the contract, because only one of us still has duties remaining to be performed. My soon-to-be-sacked counselor must provide some consideration (such as giving me back my money), or he must somehow have detrimentally changed his position in reliance on our agreement (such as leaving his commune in Oregon to teach me the ways of carrot and cabbage), or he must be able to prove that I intended to give him the money as a gift. If one of these three situations can be proved, then my counselor can rescind his obligation under the contract.

Another device for avoiding contractual responsibilities is a novation. In this procedure a party to a contract is replaced by a third party who agrees to assume the original party's duties under the contract. This substitution can be made only with the consent of the other original party, because that party will naturally be very concerned about the ability of the new party to perform the duties of the other original party. If I finance the purchase of a sleek, wood-burning station wagon and agree to pay the seller $200 a month until the balance is paid in full, we would have a novation if I brought in someone else who agreed to assume the obligation of making the monthly payments. Of course, the new party would have to be acceptable to the seller. It is unlikely that the seller would be very enthusiastic if I offered a thief as my substitute, however, even if the thief promised to burgle enough homes each month to make the payments. Because the seller would want to have someone a little more financially stable, she would be within her rights to refuse to allow the thief to take over my duties or to agree to discharge me from the contract.

An accord and satisfaction differs from a novation in that the former substitutes a new agreement for the old while the latter substitutes a new party for the old. The parties to an accord already have an existing valid agreement; the accord is a new agreement intended to replace the old agreement. It must be supported by consideration because something of value must be given so that the party promising to perform the accord can be relieved of its obligations under the original agreement. Satisfaction occurs when the promisor actually fulfills its new duties. As a result, it is the satisfaction (performance) of the accord (the substituted agreement) and not the formation of the accord that discharges the promisor's contractual obligations.

The reason that consideration must be given in order to support an accord is that the party seeking the accord is trying to be relieved of its obligations under the original agreement. In effect, that party must offer something of value to "buy" its way out of the original agreement (or at least buy the right of the other party to enforce the terms of the original agreement) and thereby induce the opposing party to agree to a new agreement having significantly different terms. If my original agreement with Ted Racket, a local tennis pro, called for me to pay $50 a lesson for a set of ten lessons, my realization after the first lesson that I probably would not be playing at Wimbledon that year (owing to my inability to hit the ball over the net, even though I could bean players in adjacent courts with deadly accuracy) might prompt me to try to get out of my agreement by offering Ted some money to cancel our remaining lessons. I might offer him $100 to tear up the contract and spare the lives of local tennis aficionados. Even though Ted might not like the idea of losing the money due under our original agreement, the increasingly vocal complaints by players on adjoining courts might cause him to suggest that we make a new agreement for a reduced number of lessons (four lessons at $50 each). In exchange, I would pay him $100 to kill the original agreement. Our new agreement would be the accord; it would be satisfied once Ted gave me four lessons and I paid him $300.

Before the accord is satisfied, it is executory (unperformed). If there is no explicit agreement allowing for the accord to be substituted for the original agreement, then the party owed the performance may sue the other party either on the accord or on the original agreement. In other words, if Ted and I made our agreement that I should take four lessons from him, he would still be able to sue me on the original ten lesson agreement if our new agreement did not expressly provide that it was a substitute for the original agreement. Of course this right to choose which agreement to sue on would disappear once it became clear which agreement we were actually performing. (If I completed six lessons at $50 each, it would be obvious that we were following the terms of our original agreement and not the accord.)

Another way for a party to get out of a contract is for the opposing party to voluntarily divest itself of the ability to perform the agreement. This prospective inability to perform excuses the performance of the innocent party once it becomes clear that the breaching party is not capable of fulfilling its contractual obligations. The innocent party is then free to sue the breaching party for damages. What is not so clear is what happens if the breaching party regains the ability to perform its obligations. The outcome seems to depend on whether the innocent party has changed its position in reliance on the apparent inability of the breaching party to perform the contract or whether the breaching party regains the ability to perform its obligations before its performance is due under the terms of the original agreement. If I agree on March 1 to sell my extensive collection of garden tools to you with actual delivery to take place on March 15, but then I turn around and physically convey them to the local ladies gardening club on March 5, I would have voluntarily divested myself of the ability to fulfill my original agreement with you. Consequently, you would be entitled to suspend your performance (paying me) and, after March 15, you would also be entitled to sue me for damages. You could not sue me for damages before March 15 even though you learned of my action on March 10, because my performance is not due until March 15. Detrimental reliance comes into play if you have incurred specific costs in reliance upon my promise to convey the goods to you, such as outfitting your garage with a rack to hold all of your new purchases. By incurring these costs, you would then be excused from performing your obligation and would be discharged from the contract. You would also be able to sue me for the costs of the rack to restore you to the position you held before you made the mistake of dealing with an untrustworthy fellow such as myself.

If I somehow reacquire the goods from the ladies gardening club before March 15, then in some jurisdictions I would be able to convey the goods to you and hold you to your promise to pay me for them. Other jurisdictions hold that an absolute breach is committed once I voluntarily divest myself of the ability to perform the contract. Even if I am able to recover the goods before the due date, I would not be able to enforce the original agreement.

The Uniform Commercial Code, which is the model for the commercial transaction statutes of most states, does not allow one party to terminate an agreement automatically when the other party appears to have given up its ability to perform the agreement. It does permit the aggrieved party to ask for adequate assurances from the other party and, if such assurances are not given within a reasonable time, to treat the contract as having been breached, thus enabling the party to sue for damages. Although there is no clear guidelines as to what grounds justify requests for adequate assurances, such requests are arguably justified whenever the insecure party reasonably fears that the goods might not be delivered. This imprecise standard means that we must ask whether it is reasonable under the circumstances to suspect that the goods will not be delivered. The same standard is used to decide whether the assurances given in return are adequate. In any event, if the insecure party demands but is not given adequate assurances of performance, that party may suspend its own performance until the requested assurances are given. If the assurances are not given for some commercially reasonable period, such as thirty days, the contract is treated as having been repudiated.

If I agree to buy a truckload of nails from Edward Nail, the proprietor of The Nail Factory so as to augment my personal collection of nails, I would probably be entitled to demand adequate assurances from Edward that he will in fact perform the contract, if he signs a contract with a major construction company, and agrees to sell all of his nails to them. I would also be entitled to adequate assurances if Edward's disgruntled workers go on strike (demanding that they be paid with money instead of nails as had been the traditional practice) and his production schedule becomes disrupted, or if all the other nail producers are vaporized by invading aliens from outer space thus causing everyone in the world to turn to The Nail Factory for nails at vastly inflated prices. Each of these situations would cause me to have some reasonable doubt that Edward would be able to perform the terms of our agreement, so I might write him a letter requesting that he assure me that he will still perform his duties under the contract. If he refused to assure me within a commercially reasonable time that his performance would be forthcoming, I would be entitled to treat the contract as breached and sue him for damages.

A party's responsibility to perform a contract may also be excused if a change in circumstances after the agreement is made makes that performance impossible. The excuse lies in the fact that the parties made an agreement but did not contemplate that some event would occur that would completely alter the balance of risks and duties in the arrangement. The doctrine of impossibility is applicable only if the intervening event is not reasonably foreseeable by the parties and it makes performance by at least one party impossible. In such circumstances, the duties of the parties would be discharged and any benefits previously conferred would be returned. It is important to point out that the performance does not have to be absolutely impossible in order for the defense to apply. However, the unforeseen event should significantly alter the obligations that had been assumed by the parties when they made their agreement.

How does one decide whether an event is foreseeable or not? Events such as acts of God, crimes by third parties, war, the death of one of the parties, the destruction of the subject matter of the contract, or even a subsequent declaration by the legislature that the particular transaction is illegal are considered to be unforeseeable. Although anything that we can contemplate is arguably foreseeable, it is clear that these situations involve circumstances where the ability of the parties to control the events is minimal. Other events that are arguably as uncontrollable as those listed above such as strikes, shortages, and inflated prices are considered foreseeable because they fall within the general fluctuations of a market economy. Changes in market prices are always considered foreseeable even if the magnitude of change is much greater than even the most wildly hallucinating economists could have imagined.

If I am convinced that there is going to be a great shortage of potatoes and I buy a one-year futures contract on ten tons of potatoes at a dollar per bushel, I will be greatly disturbed if, over the next twelve months, the value of potatoes plummets to one cent per bushel. It would be very nice if I could wriggle out of my contractual obligations by asserting the doctrine of impossibility, since no one could foresee such a drop in the value of spuds, but I would not get very far with that argument. Every market transaction involves winners and losers, and a great deal of the efficiency of the free market system would be impaired if we honored only transactions in which everybody came out ahead. Certainly if the tables were turned and I had profited hugely at the expense of some poor soul, I would not want to excuse her from the contract just because she argued that the adverse shift in spud prices was unforeseeable.

Even though an event is unforeseeable, the parties may still allocate the risk of its occurrence in any way they see fit. In other words, they might decide who is to bear the risk of destruction of the subject matter due to an act of God or an outbreak of hostilities, so that the contract is not discharged even if the intervening event is unforeseeable. This allocation of risks serves notice as to who pays for the damaged or destroyed goods should such an event occur.

The doctrine of impossibility does not excuse a party's performance if it is still possible for that party to give partial performance. If I contract to sell ten barrels of fish to a fish market, but a meteorite falls out of the sky the next day and lands on five of the barrels, I am still obliged to supply the five remaining barrels, for which I will receive proportionately reduced compensation. If five of the barrels are stolen by renegade elves, I am still responsible for delivering the five remaining barrels. If the elves suddenly have a change of heart and return the stolen barrels, then I am obligated to deliver these barrels as well. My performance would only be excused if circumstances had somehow changed so that it was no longer feasible for me to make the delivery because the fish began to smell so bad that no carrier would agree to transport them).

In a contract in which the goods (such as the ten barrels) have been specifically identified, I am excused from performing the contract if the goods are destroyed before the risk of loss has passed to the purchaser (such as when the barrels are delivered to the fish market). Such a situation arises only if the language of the agreement indicates with some particularity that my ten barrels are the ones to be sold. If instead I had five thousand barrels filled with fish and ten were destroyed, the contractual reference to ten barrels by itself would not be sufficient so as to enable me to claim the defense of impossibility of performance. I would still have to collect ten additional barrels and ship them over to the market. A different result would occur if the contract referred to the only ten fish-laden redwood barrels I possessed. If all my other barrels were oak, the destruction of those ten redwood barrels would enable me to avoid the contract, because those ten barrels were specifically identified in the contract.

The parties to a contract often make assumptions about certain conditions that they expect will either hold constant or not occur for the duration of the agreement. The doctrine of impossibility may be offered to extinguish contractual duties when, for example, conditions that are not expected to occur do occur and cause the performance to become extremely difficult. This standard does not require that the performance be impossible to render but that the surrounding circumstances be so radically different from those originally contemplated by the parties that to compel the parties to perform the agreement would cause extraordinary hardship.

A party's performance is also excused when the other party communicates her repudiation of the contract before his performance is due. This anticipatory repudiation of the agreement is usually made when the repudiating party gives notice directly to the party to whom the performance is owed. Once the innocent party receives word of the repudiation, he is entitled to suspend his own performance and to treat the agreement as breached thus enabling him to sue for damages. However, the innocent party also assumes responsibility for minimizing the damages resulting from the breach.

If I make an agreement with the Glucose Confectionary Company to purchase chocolates for a fund-raising dinner to benefit charities helping very wealthy people to cope with the pressures of modern life, the news that I have contracted some contagious respiratory disease three days before the gala affair might cause all of my guests to cancel their plans to come to the dinner. In such a catastrophic situation, I would want to avoid any costs that I could and thereby minimize the financial damage this dinner will inflict on my savings account, since only a few hungry journalists are expected to show up. Consequently, I might call up the Glucose Confectionary Company and tell them that I want to cancel my order. Given the short notice, they probably will have already made at least some of the chocolates. As a result, I might tell them that I am repudiating the agreement, even though my performance (my payment for the chocolates) is not due until their delivery on the night of the dinner. My repudiation would enable the Glucose Confectionary Company to sue me for damages and suspend their own performance; it would also impose upon them a duty not to inflate their sunk costs by making any more chocolates for me. As with other situations when one party demonstrates a prospective inability to perform, my repudiation of the contract may be withdrawn prior to the date my performance is due, so long as the Glucose Confectionary Company did not somehow change its position in the interim based on my repudiation.

In the case of installment contracts, it used to be the case before the Uniform Commercial Code was adopted that if one of the shipments arrived in unacceptable condition, the purchaser could treat the entire installment contract as having been materially breached and sue for damages. The Uniform Commercial Code took a more practical point of view: It allowed the buyer to claim a material breach of the entire contract only when an unacceptable installment significantly impaired the value of the entire contract. In other circumstances when an installment delivery is unacceptable but does not threaten the value of the other installments, the buyer may sue only for the damages caused by the defects in that particular installment.

For example, my Aunt Agatha might order twelve shipments of dates from the Exotic Fruit Company, to be delivered at monthly intervals for the next year. If one of Aunt Agatha's shipments of dates is rotten, it will not entitle her to cancel the agreement but merely to bring an action for the replacement cost of that installment. A different result might occur if one of the dates were contaminated and made Aunt Agatha so sick that she was never able to look at another date again. In this case, the defect in that date materially impaired the value of the entire contract to Aunt Agatha because she can no longer eat dates without suffering great emotional trauma. However, Aunt Agatha could conceivably waive her right to cancel the contract under the circumstances if, despite the shortcomings of the contaminated dates, she continued to accept additional monthly shipments and neglected to give a timely notice of cancellation.

A party's contractual obligations may also be extinguished if some unforeseen event so alters the circumstances under which the agreement was originally formed that its underlying objective is frustrated. In order for the defense of frustration of purpose to apply, the event must have been unforeseen at the time the contract was formed. Furthermore, the event must be one that essentially robs the contract of its expected value. If I rent a hotel room at five times the normal rate because it has a superb view of the road on which the Potato Festival Parade will pass on National Potato Day, it is reasonable to suppose that the only reason I am paying this excessive rate is because I want to see the parade. Unfortunately, I am not destined to see the newly crowned Miss Spud on the lead float because the day before the parade is scheduled to take place, the building housing all the parade floats burns down causing the parade to be cancelled.

The cancellation of the parade destroys the value of my agreement with the hotel (even though I can still stay in the hotel room and enjoy its plush polyester furniture and the fine paintings that are nailed to the walls). In such a situation, I could argue that I should not be held to the terms of the original agreement since my only reason for renting the room at five times the normal rate was to see the parade; I certainly would not have paid so much money simply to spend the night in that hotel. The court would have to determine whether the intervening act was foreseeable (probably not in this case, especially if the fire was started by a bolt of lightning or arson) and whether both the hotel management and I realized that my purpose for renting the room was to see the parade (probably so, because they charged five times the normal rate and I paid it). If the court determines that the fire was unforeseeable and that both the hotel and I realized that my only reason for paying the inflated rate was to see the parade, then it might rule that the primary purpose of the contract had been frustrated and relieve me of my duty to perform. However, courts are generally reluctant to assess the value of a party's performance, so the frustration of purpose argument usually will not be successful in obtaining a discharge from the contract.

There are a number of other situations that will discharge a party's obligation to perform, including

- a bankruptcy judgment;
- an agreement by both parties to have an arbitrator decide their dispute and fashion a remedy;
- the failure by both parties to perform their duties in a timely manner;
- the occurrence of a condition subsequent that acts to discharge an absolute duty to perform;
- and the refusal by one party to accept the complete and timely performance of the other party.

Contractual duties may also be modified by agreement between the parties.

Before the adoption of the Uniform Commercial Code, any modification of a contract had to be supported by consideration (something of value), because the pre-existing duty rule prevented a party from avoiding any of the contractual duties for which it had already received some benefit and was obliged to perform. Since the party owing the performance had already been compensated for agreeing to take on those duties, it was believed that that party should have to give something of value in order to be relieved of some of those duties. Conversely, if that party was asked to take on additional significant duties not within the scope of the original agreement, then the payment of additional consideration was proper.

If my Aunt Agatha offers me $100 over the phone to come over and kill a snake that is slithering around in her basement, then our agreement would oblige me to take whatever reasonable actions are necessary to get rid of the serpent. It would not oblige me to crawl up on the roof to replace a broken television antenna in a thunderstorm, because that task has nothing to do with my agreement with Aunt Agatha to trap the snake. I would be well within my rights to demand additional compensation for going up on the roof, because that task does not fall within my pre-existing duties regarding the snake. However, I would not be able to decide unilaterally that it is enough under the terms of our agreement to call the snake several bad names or shake a stick at it, because I agreed to kill it in exchange for the money. To be released from my obligation, I would probably have to forfeit my right to receive most, if not all, of the $100.

The adoption of the Uniform Commercial Code has made it much easier for parties to certain contracts (such as those involving the sale of goods) to make good-faith modifications (those that do not significantly increase the burdens on one or both parties and thus materially alter the terms of the original agreement) without having to give additional consideration to support these changes. As a result, Aunt Agatha and I would be free to agree on minor modifications to our agreement without additional consideration being paid, such as how I should trap the snake or dispose of the remains.

CHAPTER 4

Assignments, Delegations, and Third Party Beneficiaries

How long so ever it hath continued, if it be against reason, it is of no force in law.

— Sir Edward Coke

4

Assignments

We have spoken at some length about the rights and duties of the parties to a contract. We have yet to discuss what happens when one party assigns all of its rights or delegates all of its duties under the terms of a contract to a third party that has not previously been part of the contractual relationship. As most contracts give each party certain rights and require them to perform specific duties, assignments of rights and delegations of duties usually go together. Before we proceed into the morass further, however, it would be helpful if we borrowed a definition of the word "assignment" from one of the heaviest of legal dictionaries to set the stage for our discussion. According to *Black's Law Dictionary,* an assignment is "[a] transfer or making over to another of the whole of any property, real or personal, in possession or in action, or of any estate or right therein."[1] Despite the brevity of this definition, it isolates two important features about assignments. First, an assignment involves a complete transfer of ownership of property rights so that the assignor (the one who transfers the property) does not retain any control over it. Second, assignments can be used to transfer a wide variety of properties. In fact, it is easier to enumerate the transactions that do not use assignments to transfer property rights: "Tangible property is more often transferred by possession and by instruments conveying title such as a deed or a bill of sale."[2]

Assignments are obviously very useful devices because they facilitate the transfer of contractual rights and, unless there is language to the contrary, contractual obligations. The courts favor assignments because they permit parties to reorder their legal relationships with a minimum of cost and bother. Of course, the ease with which an assignment transfers rights or property depends on how clearly the assignment clause is drafted; the less the ambiguity, the greater the likelihood that the assignment will occur without incident. This is not to say, however, that one must have a battery of lawyers to make an effective assignment. A simple statement such as "I assign all my rights in my summer home to Egbert"

[1] *Black's Law Dictionary*, 5th ed. (St. Paul: West Publishing Company, 1979), 109.

[2] *Black's*, 109.

or "I transfer all my rights in the health spa contract to Laura" will be sufficient to convey the rights to the designated party. Of course, if one wants to make an assignment containing a lot of "hereinunders" and other archaic legal phrases, then a platoon of lawyers would do very nicely.

We noted above that most assignments involve a transfer of rights and obligations unless there is language to the contrary. There is nothing to prevent the assignor from conveying only the rights and retaining the duties under the existing contract, but the powers transferred and the responsibilities retained must be clearly specified. As assignments are often made because the assigning party wishes to get out of the transaction altogether, it is presumed that both the rights and obligations are being transferred unless an alternate scheme is noted.

Before we proceed further, we must clarify the legal terms that refer to the parties involved in an assignment. The party who makes the assignment is called the assignor. The party receiving the assignment (or the right to enforce the contract) is called the assignee. The party which originally owed its performance to the assignor (but now owes it to the assignee) is called the obligor. Obligor is a strange term; it helps to think of it as referring to the party who is obligated to perform a promise. Alternatively, we can simply force ourselves to remember that the obligor is the fellow whose obligations have not changed one bit, even though the party to which he owed his performance has transferred its rights to that performance to some possibly catatonic person known only as the "assignee." Suppose you and I make an agreement in which I promise to teach you to yodel (because you want to annoy your neighbors) in exchange for your paying me $50. You might later decide to assign your rights in the contract to your cousin Annette, who has always wanted to learn how to make the hills come alive with the sound of warbling shrieks. You would be the assignor and Annette would be the assignee, since she is the one I am now obligated to teach. Because I am the one who is obligated to teach Annette how to yodel, I am the obligor.

An alert reader might ask whether Annette, who is now obligated to pay me $50 in exchange for yodeling lessons, is also an obligor. In a way, this is true, but the reader must remember that the obligor is defined as the party which is neither the assignor nor the assignee. In short, the obligor is the only remaining original party to the contract once the assignment has been made. Calling the assignee an obligor, even though she may inherit certain duties along with her assigned rights, would be inconsistent with the terminology we have previously used and would unnecessarily complicate our discussion of the contract.

Although we spoke of the type of language necessary to make a valid assignment, we should focus on the elements that constitute an effective assignment. First, the assignor must clearly indicate that he intends to transfer his entire interest in the property or contract to the assignee. This transfer requires that the assignor convey his rights (so that he is no longer legally obligated under the contract) to the assignee who must then indicate either by words or conduct that she accepts the assignment. The acceptance of the assignment cannot be automatically presumed when the assignment has some value, because we want the assignee to be fully aware of what rights and duties she is actually agreeing to accept. We certainly do not want to permit people to go around freely assigning their interests in properties of questionable value without allowing the assignee to reject the assignment; I would not be very happy to hear that you had assigned to me your rights in land that had served as a chemical dump for many years and was now the subject of a multimillion dollar personal injury lawsuit by the inhabitants of a nearby town. The value of the property would probably be greatly outweighed by the potential legal liability. I would not want to have it forced on me and would reject the attempted assignment in the strongest possible terms.

Consideration is not required to support an assignment. An assignment may be gratuitous because it does not involve the exchange of one promise for another but instead a transfer of property rights that may be made unilaterally. The assignee plays no role in the formation of the initial agreement between the assignor and the obligor and, as a result, does not make any promise or agree to shoulder any burden to make that original agreement possible. The assignee is like a bystander watching two people (the original contractual parties) haggle over the price of a gourd in a Middle Eastern marketplace. Because gourd supplies are tight owing to an upcoming gourd festival, the seller, whose stock has been depleted, is taking paid orders for gourds he expects to receive later that day. Once the deal is struck, the buyer pays his money and is issued an invoice that he must bring back later to obtain a gourd. As a result, the buyer has acquired the property rights to one of the seller's undelivered gourds, even though he must wait until the shipment is actually received by the seller before he can claim that gourd. In any event, the seller owes the buyer a gourd. He can discharge his duties under the agreement only by giving the buyer a gourd after he receives his shipment.

After a few moments, however, the buyer might decide that he does not really know what to do with a gourd (even though he might still be quite pleased with the fine bargain he made) so he might wish to get rid of it because he does not want to come back to town again and carry the gourd all the way home. At this juncture, the buyer might spot the potential assignee crouching near a fruit stand. The buyer could then saunter over to her, hand her the invoice, and say "I give to you all my rights in this claim check." Although this sentence does not contain the words "assign" or "convey," it would have the same effect, because it would indicate that the buyer intended to transfer his rights to the gourd to the assignee. Assuming that the assignee did not refuse the assignment but said "thank you," then the acceptance of the assignment could be presumed. We should note that while one can assign personal property such as gourds, "tangible property is more often transferred by possession and by instruments conveying title such as a deed or a bill of sale." [3]

Assignments do not have to be in writing to be valid. This rule is also true if we are talking about an assignment of contract rights, even though the assignor and assignee in such a situation often commit their assignment to paper to spell out more precisely the particular rights and duties that are being assigned. We recall from our discussion of the Statute of Frauds that certain types of transactions must be evidenced by a written agreement. For example, the assignment of a lease in excess of one year or the assignment of land would have to be in writing. Because personal possessions are often transferred as gifts, we do not think of them as assignments, even though assignments and gifts are similar.

Because an assignment involves the transfer of contract rights or actual property, the question often arises as to when the assignor gives up the power to revoke the assignment. In other words, how long does the assignor have the legal right to change his or her mind? Lawyers use slightly more technical language; they ask when the assignee's rights in the contract have vested. This is not an idle question; if the assignment itself is valuable, the assignor may have second thoughts and try to reclaim it. The situation may be further complicated if the assignee has in turn conveyed the property to another party.

In general, an assignment may be revoked by the assignor. However, this rule is riddled with excep-

[3] *Black's*, 109.

tions. If the assignor has received something of value in exchange for making the assignment, then he or she cannot revoke the transfer. If I have a long-term lease on a valuable storefront property, my assignment of the lease to you would become irrevocable once you paid me a fee in exchange for my agreeing to transfer it to you. Once consideration is given for the assignment, the transaction becomes analogous to an outright purchase and my refusal to carry out my part of the bargain would be a material breach.

Another exception occurs when the assignor's promise to make the assignment causes the assignee to incur significant costs in reliance on that promise. If my promise to assign to you my winter time-share week at the Good Times Ski Resort in Sleepy Falls, Idaho, causes you to go out and buy a new ski outfit and skis, then you could argue that any later attempt by me to withdraw the assignment should not be permitted, because you incurred substantial expenses based solely on my promise to assign the time-share. Because we want to encourage people to keep their promises, the assignment would be enforced.

An assignment also becomes irrevocable if the assignor gives the assignee some legally recognized symbol of the right being assigned. If I assign my savings account to the lovely Ingrid Engebrettsen, my long-time physical therapist, my assignment would become binding when the passbook is delivered to her. The passbook is the physical symbol of my account, and my delivery of it to Ingrid creates the presumption that I intended to transfer my rights to that account to her.

An assignment also becomes irrevocable if the obligor (the one who originally owed performance to the assignor) performs for the assignee. If I promise to sell my collection of plastic drinking glass coasters to you, but you assign your right to purchase the coasters to your brother, then your assignment would become irrevocable once I completed the transaction with your brother. In a sense, we are rehashing the detrimental reliance argument, because both I (as the obligor) and your brother (as the assignee of your rights in the contract) have relied on your conveyance of the rights. It would be absurd if, after I have sold the coasters to your brother, you could change your mind and compel your brother to give them to you or force me to get them back from your brother so that I could then sell them to you. We want to promote certainty and regularity in contractual relations, so we must cut off the property owner's rights when he does some act indicating that he is voluntarily divesting himself of the property. Imagine the confusion that would result if the assignor could reclaim his property whenever he felt like being nasty; it would be impossible to make any productive use of the property because the current possessor could never be sure that the assignor would not come back and demand the property be returned.

Even if an assignment does not become irrevocable for one of the reasons mentioned above, it may be revoked by operation of law if the assignor is adjudged bankrupt. A bankruptcy candidate would want to reduce the size of his assets as much as possible before they are turned over to the court to dole out to creditors, because once the bankruptcy judgment is granted, the debtor is freed from all former financial obligations. By the same token, the courts want to prevent the debtor from dissipating his or her property so as to frustrate the claims of creditors. If no limits were placed on the debtor's ability to pass out property while the bankruptcy investigation was proceeding, then the debtor would probably give most of his or her personal property to friends (with the understanding that they would give it back later) and transfer real property such as a vacation home to a third party. Most state and federal bankruptcy laws give the courts the power to void assignments of property by the debtor to third parties for a certain number of months prior to the debtor or his creditors initiating a bankruptcy proceeding.

A revocable assignment is also terminated if the assignor dies. Although assignors often take their last breath at the most inopportune moments and thus greatly inconvenience their assignees, the courts have decided that it is generally preferable that the property be returned to the assignor's estate so that it can be distributed to deserving relatives. Perhaps the best way to consider this situation is to think of the assignor as handing the assignee the property without having yet relinquished his grasp (legally speaking) when he goes to meet his Maker. Because the assignor never fully gave up his rights in the property, it reverts to his estate when he dies.

A revocable assignment is also terminated by a notice of revocation to the assignee (when the direct approach seems more appropriate) or by a subsequent assignment to another assignee. The great thing about revocable assignments is that you can reassign the same rights as many times as you want, although it may cause you a few embarassing moments when all of your assignees gather around the punch bowl at the company holiday party and discover that you have assigned your rights to the particular property thirty-seven times. Although a few of your assignees might be impressed with your steely nerve and general arrogance, many of them may respond in a most unbecoming manner, calling you filthy names or trying to strike you. As a result, it is advisable for reasons of personal safety that an assignor not assign property rights and then revoke them by a later assignment over and over again.

We have talked about what makes an assignment irrevocable, but we have not considered the types of rights that may be assigned. In general, most rights are assignable, but there are several exceptions to this rule. If the assignment involves personal services such as giving piano lessons, then it cannot be assigned by the one who is owed the lessons because the assignor's ability to play the piano may be very different from that of the assignee (yodeling may not fall in this category since most of us already know how to scream our heads off). If you purchase ten lessons from the famous concert pianist Cleve Andrews-Brackingham (who only agreed to give the lessons because you play piano with the local symphony), then your assignment of the lessons to me, a novice, who has just mastered "Chopsticks") would not be valid, because you are a professional pianist and I am comparatively comatose on a keyboard. Even though I might be very enthusiastic about learning to play such classics as "Happy Birthday" and "Mary Had A Little Lamb" under the watchful eye of Andrews-Brackingham, it is unlikely that he would be very pleased to find that his agreement to work with a professional pianist had been assigned to someone who does not know the difference between a chord and a cord. Andrews-Brackingham, who is admittedly a snob, would be able to argue successfully that he agreed only to give lessons to a professional pianist and not to someone who is still learning to bang out the scales.

Another type of assignment that is not permitted is one that dramatically increases the burdens or risks to the obligor. If I signed an output contract with a local crafts store to supply them with all the cat fur they require, then I have decided that I can fulfill their potential requirements based on their existing demand for fur. I have sixteen cats who shed fur twelve hours a day and they are able to produce the desired amount of product. The situation would change completely, however, if the crafts store assigns the contract to a global fabrics firm with an insatiable demand for cat fur. Even if I comb my cats eighteen or twenty hours a day, urging them to new heights of productivity, it is unlikely that we will be able to meet the vastly increased requirements of this fabrics conglomerate. Although I might be able to meet their demands if I went out and purchased six thousand additional cats, I really do not have the room for that many felines in my home. Furthermore, it would be absurd for me to be required to incur huge increases in costs simply because the party that I originally agreed to supply with fur assigned their rights in the contract to someone whom I had never agreed to deal with. Because requirements and output contracts are constrained by good faith considerations, I would not be required to continue supplying the assignee with cat fur, because its requirements are vastly different from those of the crafts store that I originally agreed to supply.

The same type of reasoning applies if the crafts shop assigns the contract to the financially-anemic Gyro Yarn Company, which is owned by a mentally disturbed fellow named Vic Gyro who believes that he is constitutionally entitled to pay all of his suppliers with supermarket trading stamps. Because of his unorthodox payment system, Vic has very few suppliers who are willing to lend him credit and even fewer customers. Since the contract has been assigned to a fellow who is unlikely to pay me for my cat fur in any internationally recognized currency, the likelihood that Vic will perform his obligations under the contract would be significantly less than would have been the case had I still been dealing with the crafts shop. Consequently, Vic would not be able to enforce the contract and I would be free to peddle my wares to more financially stable companies.

When the assignment of a contract substantially increases the risk to the obligor, the assignment will not be permitted. If the obligor is the Handy Dandy Construction Company and it has promised to build a hydroelectric dam for the government of Switzerland in exchange for the latter's promise to pay it the equivalent of $50 million in Grade AAA securities, it is reasonable to suppose that the company accepted the securities due to their high financial rating (which would suggest a relatively remote possibility of default). If the Swiss government later changed its mind and decided that it did not need another dam and assigned the contract to the government of Azerubi (an impoverished desert kingdom populated by wandering tribes and sandbox merchants), the Handy Dandy company would have a completely different view of the financial risks involved, as it would now have to accept the equivalent of $50 million in Grade D Azerubi government securities. Unlike the Swiss government, the Azerubi monarchy has been broke for decades. Consequently, there would appear to be a significantly greater risk that the assignee (the Azerubi crown) would not pay Handy Dandy for building a dam (assuming that a flowing river can be found) when compared to the assignor (the Swiss government). Certainly the obligor (Handy Dandy) did not envision doing business with such a poor credit risk; the substantial increase in risk would enable the company to argue successfully that the assignment was impermissible and that it should be released from its contractual obligations.

We should point out that while vested rights in existing contracts or future rights in existing contracts (such as the right to receive royalties from future sales of a book) can be assigned, the assignment of future rights in future contracts is prohibited. For example, I cannot assign my rights to the property that I expect my Aunt Agatha to bequeath to me in her will, because my interest is not vested at present and is at best speculative. One must have an existing right to assign before one can actually assign it. I cannot assign my share of my Aunt Agatha's estate until I actually become one of her heirs at the time of her death.

Many states prohibit the assignment of alimony, child support, pensions, or wages because these income interests are viewed as being essential to the financial stability of their beneficiaries. We want to protect the vested income interests of divorced mothers and their children, retired persons (who have fixed incomes), and working people who are solely dependent on their weekly paychecks. Even if they want to assign these income rights, such assignments will not be permitted because the courts want people to avoid encumbering themselves with excessive financial obligations and thus impairing their abilities to support themselves in the future.

Contracts often contain clauses barring either party from assigning their rights in the contract. Although the language of these clauses is often quite broad, the courts tend to interpret the clauses narrowly. If the clause says that the contract will be void if it is assigned, for example, the contract will actually become voidable at the option of the obligor if it is assigned. One reason for requiring that the obligor affirmatively void the contract in such a situation is that we do not want to have it terminate automatically if it has been mistakenly assigned. Similarly, if the contract says that any assignment of the contract will be void, it will again be treated as being voidable at the option of the obligor. These prohibitions against assignment do not bar the transfer of contractual rights by operation of law such as a court judgment.

We must now consider the three situations in which the assignee or the assignor may institute legal proceedings to compel the performance of an assigned contract. The first situation arises when the assignee sues the obligor (the one who owes the performance to the assignee) to compel the obligor to fulfill his obligations under the contract. Because an assignment is a complete transfer of rights in which no residual power is retained by the assignor, the assignee "steps into the shoes" of the assignor and may enforce the contract to the extent that it could have been enforced by the assignor. This means that the obligor can assert any defenses that existed before the contract was assigned, such as having been fraudulently induced to sign the original agreement. However, the obligor cannot assert any defenses that arise after the contract has been effectively assigned. Once the assignee's right to the obligor's performance "vests," subsequent defenses will not act to discharge the obligor's duty to perform.

The obligor can argue that he should not have to perform his duties if the assignor (or the assignee) failed to fulfill her part of the bargain. If my Aunt Agatha and I agree that I will personally supervise the refurbishing of her polecat farm subject to the condition that I be paid a $5,000 retainer before beginning work, Aunt Agatha's failure to fulfill this condition would provide me with a defense for withholding my own performance. If Aunt Agatha later sells the polecat farm (because she has become interested in breeding racing snails) and assigns our agreement to the new owner, Mr. Tibbs, he will be no more able to compel me to fulfill the contract than my Aunt Agatha if he refuses to pay the retainer. Mr. Tibbs cannot be assigned rights greater than those that were originally held by Aunt Agatha.

The obligor will also be excused from performing the assigned contract if he performs his obligations before he learns that the contract has been assigned. We do not want to discourage parties from carrying out their contractual obligations by subjecting them to potential multiple liabilities, so the receipt of notice of the assignment serves as the marker as to whether the obligor's performance should be rendered to the assignor or the assignee. If the obligor is somewhat masochistic, however, and insists on performing for the assignor after he has received notice of the assignment, he will still be required to perform for the assignee. The law will not protect people who do stupid things when they know they should behave otherwise.

In many types of consumer transactions, the purchaser (obligor) will be asked to waive certain defenses (though many states have consumer protection laws prohibiting such contract clauses) that he might otherwise be able to assert against the seller or her assignee. Here we must distinguish between personal defenses that may be waived and real defenses that may not be waived. Personal defenses are those that do not adversely impact upon the legal validity of the contract itself. They include misrepresentations regarding the nature of the goods or the value of the consideration being paid. Real defenses, by contrast, arise from legal defects in the contract itself. They include infancy (a minor may disaffirm a contract before reaching the age of majority), incapacity (a party does not have to be declared legally incompetent to use this defense), duress, misrepresentations as to the nature of the contract itself, the forgery of the obligor's signature, illegal subject matter, and any judicial discharge of the obligor's contractual responsibilities such as a bankruptcy decree.

If I purchase a color television from Television World and sign a sales contract stating that I agree to waive any defenses that I might otherwise be entitled to raise against the seller or her assignee, the extent to which I have given up my rights to raise these defenses will depend on whether they are personal or real defenses. If the sales contract was purportedly for a color television but it contained some extremely small print saying that I had agreed to buy a vast assortment of electronic products from Television World next month, then I could argue that the contract itself was tainted by fraud because I had been led to believe it was for the sale of a television set only. When a buyer is tricked into signing a contract with terms vastly different from those that he believes are contained in it, the contract itself is fundamentally flawed because there is no mutual assent between the parties. In addition, the element of fraud is present because the seller buried onerous conditions in unreadable type and did not inform me of their existence. Because fraud in the execution of the contract permits me to raise a real defense, the fact that I agreed to waive all my defenses in the sales contract is irrelevant; real defenses cannot be waived. If, on the other hand, the seller had said that my color television contains the latest in solid-state technology when its interior actually consists of a jumble of vacuum tubes and soldered wires, then my waiver might be binding, because a misrepresentation regarding the product itself would allow me to raise a personal defense. It is the product itself and not the contract that is arguably defective or, at least, misrepresented.

Whether the assignee can proceed against the assignor depends on whether the assignment may be revoked by the latter. If the assignment is freely revocable, then the assignee has no right to institute legal proceedings, because he has no vested right to the obligor's performance. If, on the other hand, the assignor irrevocably assigns her rights in the contract to the assignee and then somehow interferes with the assignee's or the obligor's subsequent efforts to perform the contract, then the assignee could sue the assignor for interfering with his contractual relations.

When a party assigns her rights in a contract in exchange for something of value (money), she implicitly promises or warrants

- that the rights she is assigning are what she asserts them to be;
- that there are no undisclosed defenses that the obligor may assert against either the assignor or the assignee to avoid his contractual obligations; and
- that the assignor will not wrongfully interfere with the assignee's rights.

However, these warranties do not extend to anyone to whom the assignee might later assign the contract. The assignor is not presumed to make (in the absence of explicit language to the contrary) any guarantees regarding the ability of the obligor to perform. If you assign your rights to receive a rare mohogany pigeon roost for $100 to me, you are not guaranteeing that the obligor will actually convey the antique to me if I pay him. You are simply conveying your rights to sue the obligor for not performing his obligations under the contract. I have no legal right to sue you if the obligor fails to perform his duties.

As far as the assignor's rights against the obligor are concerned, the actions that she can take will depend on whether she has irrevocably assigned her rights to the contract. If the contract is revocable, then the assignor can reassume her status as the party to whom the obligor owes his performance by revoking the assignment to the assignee. Alternatively, the assignor can reassign the rights to a different party, automatically revoking the first assignment. If the assignee paid consideration for the assignment, however, then the assignor will have no power to withdraw the assignment.

Chapter 4

Delegations

Although most assignments of rights also involve delegations of duties, we have dealt primarily with the abilities of assignors and assignees to enforce their rights in a contract. We have paid less attention to the transfer of responsibilities or obligations under a contract. As with assignments, we must deal with three parties, but because we are now talking about the transfer of duties instead of rights, we must use a different terminology to refer to each of the three parties involved. The party to whom the performance is owed is called the obligee. The party who owes that performance under the contract is called the obligor. Once the obligor delegates duties under the contract to a third party, the obligor will be known as the delegator (the one who delegates the duties). The third party accepting that delegation of duties will be known as the delegatee.

A delegation of duties is somewhat different than an assignment of rights in so far as the residual liability of the delegator is concerned, because the delegator remains secondarily liable for performing the delegated duties should the delegatee be unable or unwilling to perform. We recall that in the case of an irrevocable assignment, the assignor transfers all his rights in the contract to the assignee and is thus excused from the contractual relationship. One reason for this difference in legal liability is that when the assignment of rights is involved, we are dealing with a right to something of value as opposed to an obligation to perform some duty. We usually do not have to worry about a party exercising a right to something of value, but we often have to concern ourselves with whether a party will perform some duty that it has agreed to undertake. In short, we do not have to worry about a child eating a piece of candy, but we often have to order the child to take prescribed medicine, because the latter is regarded as unpleasant while the former is regarded with pleasure.

To have an effective assignment, the assignor must indicate that she intends to convey her rights in the contract to the assignee. To have an effective delegation the delegatee must act in such a manner to indicate that he agrees to accept the delegation of duties from the delegator. The fact that the delegator intends to delegate her duties to a third party is of no consequence if the third party has no interest in assuming those duties. If the situation were otherwise, then we would have delegators running around delegating their contractual responsibilities to innocent third parties. If I had agreed to ship ten truckloads of bricks to a retailer, it would be very nice for me if I could run up to an old woman feeding birds in a park and delegate my duty to ship the bricks to her. Not only would she probably be very bewildered by a strange man declaring that she was his delegatee, but she would probably not be a brick supplier and would not know how to fulfill her newly acquired duties. For my delegation to be effective, the old woman would have to accept in some unequivocal manner the delegation of the duties. If it turned out later that she was hard of hearing and had mistakenly thought that I had asked her to be my fiancée, not my delegatee, then there would be no valid delegation, because the old woman did not manifest an intent to accept my duties under the contract.

As with assignments of rights, most contractual duties may be delegated except those that would materially alter the performance that had been contracted for in the original agreement. If my Aunt Agatha hires the well-known artist Leo Nardo to paint her portrait for $1,000, but Nardo later has a change of heart and delegates his duties under the contract to one of his assistants, Michael Angelo, who specializes in painting by numbers, then Aunt Agatha would be able to cancel the contract. Only Leo Nardo could paint in the manner that was envisioned by Aunt Agatha in the original agreement; his style is unique and could not be replicated by one of his assistants. In short, there is no way that Aunt Agatha's expectations under the contract could be fulfilled once Leo Nardo delegated his duties.

In general, duties are nondelegable only so long as the contract is premised on the unique abilities of the obligor.[4] One might think that construction contracts would also be nondelegable since every builder builds homes and buildings using slightly different techniques, but construction contracts have been held to be delegable because when you sign a contract with a builder it is generally assumed that employees of the builder will do the actual work. One cannot argue that the Sinkhole Building Company is unable to delegate its duties to build a ranch house under a

[4] Gifis, *Law Dictionary,* 124.

contract, because it usually hires subcontractors to do more specialized tasks, such as the roofing, the plumbing, and the wiring. There can be no expectation of a unique performance, because so many different parties will be involved in completing that performance.

We recall that contracts often contain clauses prohibiting the assignment of rights or the delegation of duties. In the case of assignments, we saw that even though the contractual language might state that any assignment would render the contract void, the usual effect was to make the contract voidable at the option of the other party. The same result generally occurs when a delegation of duties is made, even though the contract forbids the same. Such a delegation does not automatically void the contract, but it gives the option of disaffirming the contract to the obligee (the one who is owed the performance). If the obligee fails to exercise the right to void the contract within a reasonable time, then her acquiescence will be presumed and the delegation will be permitted.

After the duties are effectively delegated, the delegatee becomes directly liable to the obligee and may be sued if he fails to perform his duties. Because the delegator remains secondarily liable, however, the obligee may choose to proceed directly against her instead of the delegatee when the latter fails to perform his duties. If the delegatee satisfactorily performs the delegated duties, however, both he and the delegator will be discharged from any further obligations. Because the delegator remains liable on the delegated contract, she may sue the delegatee to compel him to perform his obligations or to obtain money damages in lieu of specific performance.

If I hire Stanley Scrubb, a well-known cleaner of septic tanks, to rehabilitate the drainage system of Barrymore Estate, but he later delegates his duties under our contract (because he is backlogged with appointments) to a competitor, Herb Rooter, the latter's failure to do the job properly would enable me to sue Herb for specific performance (to complete the job) or for money damages, or to proceed directly against Stanley. Even though I could sue them together, I would only be entitled to recover a single award of money damages, because a fundamental maxim of contract law is that injured parties should be made whole. They are not entitled to make excess profits on their lawsuits above the amount of damages that they have actually suffered, though there are a few lawyers who have not accepted this view completely.

Third Party Beneficiaries

The assignment of contractual rights is often confused with the creation of rights in third party beneficiaries, but they may be easily distinguished. An assignment to an assignee can be made only after a valid contract is in existence between the assignor and the obligor. A third party beneficiary contract, by contrast, involves an agreement between two parties in which the promisor agrees in the contract to render his performance not to the promisee but to a third party who may be named in the contract but is not a signatory. The third party beneficiary contract involves all three parties from the time the agreement is formed.

Before we proceed further, we should define a third party beneficiary as "persons who are recognized as having enforceable rights created in them by a contract to which they are not parties and for which they give no consideration. These persons can be loosely grouped into two classes:

- donee beneficiaries, and
- creditor (or obligee) beneficiaries.

The third person is a donee beneficiary if the promisee who buys the promise expresses an intention and purpose to confer a benefit upon him or her as a gift in the shape of the promised performance. He or she is a creditor beneficiary if the promisee, or some other person is under an obligation (a duty or a liability) to him or her and the contract is so made that the promised performance or the making of the executory contract itself will discharge that obligation."[5]

We encounter third party beneficiary situations every day, but they are often so routine that we do not give them a second thought. If I owe my Aunt Agatha $500 because I accidentally backed my car over one of her cats and Aunt Agatha subsequently purchased a replacement tabby for $500 from the Cat House, (one of the world's most distinguished and expensive feline breeding establishments), she might tell me to pay the $500 directly to the Cat House, thereby discharging her debt as well as mine at the

[5] Corbin, *Contracts*, §774.

same time. In this case, I would be the promisor and Aunt Agatha would be the promisee to whom I owed my performance. The Cat House would be the third party beneficiary; it was the party designated by Aunt Agatha to receive my payment even though it was neither a party to our agreement nor had it given any consideration to me in exchange for my promise to pay the $500 to it. In deciding whether the Cat House is a donee beneficiary or a creditor beneficiary, we would recall that my payment is not intended to be a gift to the Cat House but to discharge Aunt Agatha's existing debt. Therefore, the Cat House is a creditor beneficiary of our agreement. Donee and creditor beneficiaries are discussed in greater detail below.

Whether the third party can actually bring a suit to compel the promisor's performance depends on whether the promisee intended the beneficiary to have legal rights. In other words, we must determine whether we have an intended or an incidental beneficiary, because only the former may sue the promisor to compel its performance. An intended beneficiary is usually specified by name or some other identifying criteria in the original agreement by the promisee. An incidental beneficiary, by contrast, is one who the promisee did not intend to benefit but who is able to enjoy the promisor's performance by being in the right place at the right time. We have already alluded in the above example to an intended beneficiary; my Aunt Agatha intended to confer a benefit on the Cat House by having me pay them directly to satisfy my debt to her and her debt to the Cat House simultaneously. Because the Cat House is an intended beneficiary, it has the right to institute legal proceedings to collect its debt from the promisor (me). The Cat House would be an incidental beneficiary if I had promised only to give the payment to Aunt Agatha; it would then be up to her to discharge her own debt with the Cat House. In this case, I would not have made any promise to pay the Cat House directly; it would have no immediate interest in our agreement even though Aunt Agatha plans to forward my money to it.

We have shown that third party beneficiaries may be distinguished by whether the promisee intends to confer a benefit on them. We must further divide this class of beneficiaries into donee and creditor beneficiaries. Donee beneficiaries are those parties who are the intended recipients of a gratuitous benefit (gift). In short, they are lucky enough to be given something of value not because they are owed money but because the promisee desires to confer a benefit unilaterally on them. However, the courts have tended to treat donee beneficiaries as a sort of residual category into which they have lumped all beneficiaries that did not fit neatly into the creditor beneficiary classification. If I owe you $500 for a past debt, but you happen to be in a charitable mood on the day I try to hand you the money and instead tell me to give it to the Foundation for Manic Golfers (a charitable organization established to help overly enthusiastic duffers resist the temptation to aim their shots at slower parties playing ahead of them), the Foundation would be a donee beneficiary; my payment to them would not discharge any pre-existing debt owed by you to them. I would simply be conferring a monetary benefit to them in the form of a gift, even though this action would discharge the debt I owe to you.

A creditor beneficiary, by contrast, is one to whom the promisee (you) owes a debt that can be satisfied by my paying the beneficiary directly (on your behalf) to discharge the obligation. In the above example where Aunt Agatha owed the Cat House $500, the latter is a creditor beneficiary because Aunt Agatha's request that I pay the Cat House directly and my subsequent compliance discharges Aunt Agatha's debt. In this case, she is not asking me to give the money as a gift but to satisfy her existing financial obligation. To return to our golf example, if you directed that I pay the money I owed you to the Foundation not because you desire to give it a charitable contribution but instead to pay for your two months of rehabilitative therapy there, then the Foundation would be a creditor beneficiary and my payment to them would discharge your debt.

As with the assignment of contract rights, the question often arises as to when the contracting parties can no longer alter the terms of their agreement without considering the wishes of the beneficiary. In short, we want to know when the beneficiary's rights to the promisor's performance have vested and the promisor and the promisee are no longer free to modify their agreement without the approval of the beneficiary. An assignee or third party beneficiary's rights vests when that person either

- receives notice of the assignment of rights or the creation of the third party beneficiary contract;
- acts in some overt manner to indicate assent to or acceptance of the assignment;
- or detrimentally relies on the assignment or the creation of the third party beneficiary contract.

The donee beneficiary's rights may vest in each of these three ways; the creditor beneficiary's rights vest only when there is demonstrable assent or detrimental reliance.

As with the assignment of contractual rights, we must delineate the rights and duties of the parties in a third party beneficiary agreement. Because the third party is either named or identified in the agreement as the one who is to receive the performance of the promisor, the third party beneficiary (assuming that he is not an incidental beneficiary with no legal rights to enforce the agreement) will be able to compel the promisor to fulfill his contractual obligations to the same extent that the promisee could have done so.

To return to our example, my promise to give the money I owe Aunt Agatha directly to the Cat House to discharge her debt may be enforced by the Cat House. Although the language of the original agreement between Aunt Agatha and myself will affect the ease with which the Cat House can drag me into court, the general rule is that it will be able to assert the same rights as Aunt Agatha could if I should breach our agreement. We should point out that if I had promised to pay Aunt Agatha $500 originally, but she had incurred expenses of $1,500 at the Cat House, the latter could enforce my promise only to the extent of $500, because that is all that I promised to pay to Aunt Agatha. The fact that Aunt Agatha still owes an additional $1,000 to the Cat House does not increase the liability I had originally agreed to assume. The Cat House can sue me only for $500; it will have to go after Aunt Agatha for the remainder of the debt.

Because the rights of the Cat House are derived from the original agreement between myself and Aunt Agatha, any defects in that agreement that provide me with defenses against having to pay the money to Aunt Agatha also apply to the Cat House. As a third party beneficiary, it cannot enforce our original agreement when there is a fundamental flaw in that agreement, such as fraud, duress, or illegal subject matter. We might view the contract as a bridge over which I will cross to pay Aunt Agatha her money. If the floorboards of the bridge have rotted and fallen into a deep canyon below, then I cannot cross the bridge and Aunt Agatha cannot collect the money. Needless to say, if she cannot collect the money, the Cat House, which we may assume is standing next to her with its paw out, cannot collect it either. Even though our agreement might have been perfectly legal at the time it was made, if the legislature of our state decided to make third party beneficiary agreements illegal, for example, or passed legislation that made our contract unenforceable, then Aunt Agatha would be unable to enforce our agreement. If Aunt

Agatha is unable to enforce our agreement, the third party beneficiary also will be unable to do so, because the latter's rights are essentially derived from those of the former.

We have talked about the fearful consequences that would result if I failed to perform my end of the bargain, but what would happen if Aunt Agatha did not carry out her part of the agreement? If Aunt Agatha and I had agreed that I would pay her $100 in exchange for her giving me her television set, but she told me to pay the Cat House to satisfy a pre-existing debt, what could I do if Aunt Agatha refused to hand over the television set? In this situation (assuming that Aunt Agatha and I expected to perform our obligations simultaneously), I would be excused from having to give Aunt Agatha the money since she did not give me the television set. Because she has no right to compel me to pay her directly, she cannot force me to pay her creditor. The Cat House may assert its rights only if Aunt Agatha fulfills her duties and thereby activates my obligation to make the payment.

The same type of argument would also apply if the Cat House did something to make it impossible for Aunt Agatha and I to perform our original agreement. If the owners of the Cat House broke into Aunt Agatha's mansion and ran off with her television set, she would be unable to perform her part of our agreement. Since she cannot give me the television set, she cannot compel me to pay her the money. Moreover, the Cat House would be estopped from asserting any flimsy rights it might have, because it acted in a manner that made the performance of our agreement impossible. A basic maxim of the law is that people should not profit from their wrongs. Thus, if the Cat House owners did steal the television set, the courts would not look kindly on any effort by the Cat House to assert its rights as a third party beneficiary.

The Cat House can sue my Aunt Agatha on the original obligation if I fail to perform my obligation, or if Aunt Agatha and I somehow modify our agreement to the detriment of the Cat House (assuming that its rights have vested and we are no longer entitled to modify our agreement without its approval). If the Cat House is a creditor beneficiary, it will be entitled to sue my Aunt Agatha to force her to pay her debt (unless I or someone else has agreed to be fully responsible for her debt as would be the case if there was a novation substituting another party for Aunt Agatha) if I fail to pay the money to the Cat House. But the third party beneficiary can assert only those rights that it acquired through its original agreement with Aunt Agatha; it cannot gain additional rights from the existence of my original agreement with Aunt Agatha. If I owed $500 to Aunt Agatha and she owed $300 to the Cat House, the Cat House would only be able to obtain $300 from me if I agreed to pay my debt to Aunt Agatha directly to the Cat House. It cannot collect $500 from me simply because that was the amount of my original debt owed to Aunt Agatha, nor can it assert any additional rights arising out of our agreement other than my original promise to Aunt Agatha to pay $300 to the Cat House on her behalf.

If Aunt Agatha asked me to pay the money I owed her to the Cat House in the form of a gift, (because she wants to encourage their efforts to help uncoordinated cats learn to pry the lids off of garbage cans), then the Cat House would be a donee beneficiary. It would be able to enforce a charitable pledge by Aunt Agatha, but it would be unable to hold her legally responsible if she had given no indication that she intended to give a gift. To have a valid gift, the donor must intend to give a gift and actually deliver the gift to the intended recipient. In addition, the recipient must accept the gift. If Aunt Agatha has not communicated her intent to give a gift to the Cat House, then it cannot accept the gift. As a result, it would be unable to assert a valid claim against Aunt Agatha if the gift was not made.

We must also consider what would happen if Aunt Agatha sued me to keep my promise to pay a debt she owes to a third party. If I fail to perform my part of our agreement, I will have breached my promise and Aunt Agatha could resort to normal contract remedies (to be discussed in greater detail in the next chapter) to recover the amount of the debt I owed to her (which she would presumably pay to her creditor). Aunt Agatha can recover the amount of money that I promised to pay to her creditor beneficiary (the Cat House) regardless of whether she paid her original debt. In general, Aunt Agatha can only recover the amount that I originally agreed to pay to her creditor. However, if my failure to pay the Cat House causes her to incur added damages (such as having to defend herself against a law suit brought by the

Cat House), then I might also be responsible for those additional costs since my delay arguably contributed to the initiation of the suit. If I had broken my promise to give Aunt Agatha's creditor some unique item (instead of money), such as a football autographed by Napoleon Bonaparte, then she would be able to sue me for specific performance. If she was successful, the court could order me to give her creditor the football.

Because my primary responsibility is to pay Aunt Agatha's creditor, I must be careful not to pay Aunt Agatha without requesting that the Cat House be joined as a party to our proceedings. I do not want to pay both Aunt Agatha and the creditor beneficiary for the same debt. In the case of a donee beneficiary, however, we have no debt that I have agreed to satisfy; the only solution other than specific performance is for me to give back whatever money or property that Aunt Agatha originally gave to me in exchange for my promise to perform for the donee beneficiary. If Aunt Agatha gave me $50 to take her obnoxious grandson Elvin to the zoo, but I reneged on our agreement, then Aunt Agatha can sue me to recover the $50. Although she could also seek specific performance in certain situations, such as those involving land or personal property, no court would want to supervise what would essentially be my personal service agreement to take Elvin to the zoo. As a result, the remedy of specific performance in this situation would probably be unavailable.

CHAPTER 5

Contract Remedies

"If the law supposes that," said Mr. Bumble . . . "the law is a ass—an idiot."

— Charles Dickens

5

In the best of all possible worlds, we would not have very much litigation over breached contracts. Everyone would carry out their contractual duties because they would want to do the right thing. They would not be motivated by fears that they could be dragged into court if they failed to carry out their obligations. Sadly for humankind (but fortunately for the lawyers who try such cases) we do not have such a happy state of affairs; the courts are innundated with cases involving disputes over who failed to perform their contractual duties or whether, in fact, an enforceable contract was created. Because contracts are merely instruments in which two parties set out the terms of their agreement, it is inevitable that disputes will arise over what each party is required to do or not do and what meaning may be drawn from a particular clause or paragraph. In short, contracts are no more perfect than the persons who draft them; it is unrealistic to expect that agreements can be set out in such a manner that the parties will always be satisfied with them. Disputes over who has or has not performed their duties satisfactorily will arise; the parties may then turn to an impartial arbiter such as a court to resolve the matters.

Contract remedies exist to satisfy the expectation interests of the nonbreaching innocent party by providing various ways for that party to be put in the position it would have enjoyed had the agreement been fully performed. We spoke earlier of the expectation interest being the advantage or gain that a party expects to realize from the performance of the contract by both parties. Since the courts are very concerned with promoting contractual agreements between parties and facilitating the ease with which contracts can be formed and executed, they have developed a number of remedies over the years to protect innocent parties, as well as to encourage parties considering breaching their agreements to rethink the wisdom of such a strategy.

Money damages is the most common remedy given by a court to an innocent party when a contract is breached. One reason for the popularity of money damages is that almost all property and all tangible objects can be reduced to some monetary value. Consequently, it is fairly easy for a court to order that a specific sum be paid by the breaching party to the innocent party; money is a commonly recognized medium of exchange and store of value. The situation would be much more complicated if we lived in a barter economy and two parties were involved in a law suit over the value of the breaching party's performance. Because there would be no common currency in which the assessment of value could be grounded, the parties (and the judge) would have to decide if the undelivered performance was worth a gross of eggs or five golden rings or a trunk of skunk pelts. The precedential value of such decisions would be of little help to other parties involved in contractual disputes unless the same type of property and the same type of relief were desired—a set of circumstances not likely to happen.

Because we live in a money economy, the parties to a contract may specify the value of the performance in a contract, or a judge may have recourse to various market price quotations or industry guidelines to arrive at a fair estimate of the damages that must be paid by the breaching party to make the innocent party whole again. Although the court has the power to fashion its own remedy, the parties are perfectly free to set out a particular remedy in the agreement itself. This remedy will be enforced by the court if it appears to be a fair solution given the situation that existed at the time the agreement was made. The fact that events may have transpired since the agreement was made that make the contract less advantageous to one party (presumably the breaching party) is of little importance here because we are concerned most with the perceptions that each party had regarding its duties and obligations when the contract was made and the private remedies spelled out.

When we speak of the interests of the innocent party in a breached agreement, we are speaking of three types of legal rights that the courts want to protect. The first of the three is the "restitution" interest that arises when one party conveys some property or right to another with the expectation that the other party will then perform its part of the agreement. Once the contract is breached, however, the innocent party (which conveyed the property) now has an interest in having the property returned, because the other party will not be performing the obligation that it undertook in exchange for that property. If I convey my priceless ceramic tropical drinking mug to you because you promised to give me your mother's antique five-sided brooch (which you are certain you will inherit when she dies because you peeked at her will), I would have the right to demand that you give me back my mug if you refused to give me the brooch after it became your personal property. I would have an interest in having the benefit I conferred to you restored to me so that I could be put back in the position I occupied before we made our agreement. You would have to make this restitution of the mug to me to protect yourself from being sued by me for unlawfully detaining my property.

The second interest that we want to protect is the "reliance" interest, which usually consists of any expenses a party incurred to facilitate the performance of the agreement. These expenses might include the cost of renting storage facilities to house the purchased item or perhaps buying an accessory such as a boat trailer on which the purchased item will be kept. In short, any costs that the innocent party incurred in preparing for the breaching party's performance could be considered a reliance interest. Of course, these expenses must be made in good faith; the courts will disallow any costs that were incurred simply to fatten the amount of the damages. To return to our brooch example, one of my reliance costs might be the purchase of a five-sided box to store your five-sided brooch. I probably would not have purchased such a uniquely shaped box if I had not been reasonably certain that I would soon have the brooch in my possession. If the court decided that this purchase was reasonable and foreseeable under the circumstances, then it would order you to pay me for the cost of the box if you refused to convey the brooch.

The expectation interest represents the third and final component of the possible damages that might be awarded to an innocent party. Unlike the restitution and reliance interests, which are designed to put parties back in their original positions, the expectation interest represents the assessment by the court of what is required to give the innocent party the benefit of the bargain. The benefit of the bargain is determined by considering what property or right the innocent party was trying to obtain through the agreement. If it is not practical for the court to order that the specific property itself be conveyed (perhaps because it has been destroyed or lost or stolen), then the court can determine what money damages would be appropriate to give the innocent party the benefit of its bargain.

Is there any limit to the amount of damages that can be recovered for a breached contract? Although some of our more pyrotechnically-oriented legal tacticians are quite adept at convincing juries that no amount of damages will make the innocent party whole again, they are generally quite willing to settle for a fixed dollar amount. When we consider the question of the amount of damages that may be assessed, we must look to the contract at the time it was formed to see what sorts of costs could reasonably have been expected to result from either party's failure to fulfill its obligations. In short, we must decide what damages were foreseeable at the time the parties made their agreement. If six months pass and it becomes clear that damages much greater than originally envisioned are foreseeable, that change does not permit the injured party to pad the amount of damages to which it is entitled. In summary, the courts will try to be as specific as possible by focusing on the damages that were within the contemplation of the parties at the time the agreement was made or on the damages that could be reasonably expected to flow from a breach of the agreement.

Not only must the damages flowing from a breach be foreseeable, they must also be calculable. A court must know with some certainty the amount of damages that a party has suffered. Otherwise, it will be unable to order that a particular sum be paid because it will not know whether it is undercharging or penalizing the breaching party. In many situations it is clear that damages have been caused by a party's breach, but the circumstances are such that it is impossible to put a price on the amount of the damages. If I am hired by the town of Wippleshire to build a leak-proof chemical dump which I construct using materials such as balsa wood and airplane glue instead of cement and steel and thus contaminate the town's water supply, it would be difficult to assess the exact amount of damages I should be required to pay because the townspeople might suffer illnesses in the future based on their consumption of contaminated drinking water. However, this uncertainty would not get me off the hook. The court can order me to pay the costs of cleaning the dump and the water supply. It might also order me to pay the medical bills of the Wippleshire citizens that can be reasonably attributed to their drinking contaminated water. So long as there is some acceptable means for calculating an estimate of the damages suffered, I would be required to pay money damages.

When a seller and a buyer are involved in a contract dispute, the amount of damages owed by the breaching party is usually the difference between the contract price and the market price. This rule permits the innocent party to recover the value of its expectation interest in the contract when the market price of a good diverges from the sale price. Because goods may be sold in installments or held for future delivery, it is unrealistic to expect that the market price of the good will continue to be the same as the contract price. If I agree to sell you 100 light bulbs for $100, we will have a contract for me to deliver 100 light bulbs at a dollar per bulb. If the bottom drops out of the light bulb market before I actually deliver the goods so that 100 light bulbs can be purchased for ten cents each, you may suddenly have an overwhelming desire to squirm out of our contract and buy the light bulbs from a light bulb peddler on the streetcorner. If you do breach the contract, I will be able to recover the difference between the contract price and the price for which I can resell the light bulbs elsewhere. Since the market price of light bulbs is now ten cents each, I will be able to recover ninety cents per light bulb from you or a total of $90 for the entire sale.

If the price of light bulbs rockets upward, by contrast, after we sign our contract, so that light bulbs now cost $10 each, I will now be the one with the incentive to avoid the contract. I can only make $100 if I sell the light bulbs to you under the contract, while I can earn $1,000 if I sell the goods on the open market. As I am one of those merchants who loves money more than life itself, I would probably breach the contract and hope that you did not exercise your legal rights. As in the situation when you breached the contract because you could buy the light bulbs for much less money elsewhere, my breach would enable you to recover the difference between the contract price and the prevailing market price. Since light bulbs are now so scarce that people are willing to trade their children for a box of them, it will not be difficult for you to show that my breach is due solely to my desire to make more money and not a legitimate defense such as impossibility of performance. Consequently, you would be able to recover the difference between the contract price ($100) and the price that you would have to pay on the open market for replacement bulbs ($1,000), which is $900. Of course, you would not be entitled to recover any money if the contract price and the market price were the same at the time I breached the contract, because you would be able to obtain replacement light bulbs elsewhere for the same price as called for by the contract. In such a situation, if you chose to sue me simply to show that you were not about to be pushed around by a merchant, you would probably recover only nominal or token damages.

The innocent party is also entitled to recover any incidental damages from the breaching party, such as the transaction costs associated with finding another buyer or seller and delivering the goods to that person. Another form of incidental damages might be the cost of storing the goods while the seller found another buyer, or the expenses incurred by the buyer while preparing for the receipt of the goods before the seller breached the agreement. In addition, the innocent party is entitled to recover any consequential damages that are the result of a particular situation which that party cannot otherwise avoid or alleviate through his own actions.

We spoke above of the preference many contractual parties have for fashioning their own remedies for a breach. Such remedies are usually outlined in the contract itself. For example, the parties might agree to submit any disputes regarding the terms of the contract to an arbitrator or allow the breaching party to pay a fixed sum to purchase the innocent party's right to sue him. The latter device is essentially a liquidated damages clause, which represents an agreement by the parties as to how much money the breaching party must pay the innocent party in order to be excused from further legal liability under the contract. Because of the potential for abusing liquidated damages clauses, however, the parties are not totally free to set whatever amount they wish.

A court will permit the liquidated damages clause to discharge the breaching party's obligations under the agreement only if the stated amount is a reasonable estimate of the damages that would result from a breach given the situation that existed at the time the parties made the agreement. The courts are reluctant to permit an innocent party to be paid not to sue the breaching party and thus forfeit a potentially larger recovery in the courts. Before a court will enforce a liquidated damages clause, it must determine that

- the damages from a breach of the contract were difficult to determine when the parties made their agreement, and
- the liquidated damages clause was tailored to the circumstances surrounding that particular agreement.

In other words, the courts would not permit a conglomerate such as the Global Popcorn Company to insert a liquidated damages clause for $500, for example, into all of its retail contracts regardless of the circumstances involved. Such a systematic practice would not show that the parties had contemplated what damages would arise from a breach, or that the amount was specifically tailored to the particular agreement, or that it was difficult to determine the damages resulting from a breach.

The above conditions suggest that an excessive liquidated damages clause cannot be imposed simply to punish the breaching party beyond the amount of actual damages. Punitive damages are seldom awarded in contract law because the courts are concerned primarily with giving the innocent party the benefit of the bargain or restoring both parties to their original positions. They are not so concerned with imposing an additional penalty on top of all recoverable damages. One exception to this rule occurs occasionally when the breaching party has intentionally acted in a manner calculated to injure the interests of the other party. When the courts are presented with an "evil breaching party" they will sometimes impose punitive damages to punish the breaching party for that behavior. Punitive damages have nothing to do with the subject matter or the terms of the contract but are simply a judicial device for slapping the knuckles of the breaching party with a very heavy ruler. Subject to this exception, however, the courts are generally reluctant to apply punitive damages in a contract dispute.

Even though the innocent party is the one who suffers from the breaching party's actions, the former is still required to minimize the amount of damages that the latter will have to pay for committing the breach. The innocent party is thus not permitted to inflate the amount of damages. To return to the light bulb example in which I breached the contract, you would not be justified in searching for the most expensive seller of light bulbs in the world so as to maximize the difference between the contract price

($100 per 100 light bulbs) and the existing market price that I would have to pay for my breach. If you finally purchased your 100 light bulbs from a Tibetan yak herder who sold them for $50 each, out of a shack in the shadow of Mount Everest, it would be clear that you had deliberately looked for the most expensive source of light bulbs you could find simply to increase the damages I would have to pay. Absent some sort of business justification such as an acute shortage of light bulbs (caused by a suspicious natural disaster in the form of simultaneous fires burning all the light bulb stores and factories in the world to the ground in the same night), you would probably not be able to defend your claim for damages. The court would want to know why you bought light bulbs in Tibet when you could have bought them for one-fifth the price at your neighborhood dry goods store. Because lawyers have a tendency to ask such bothersome questions at trials (when even fibbing about insignificant facts can result in a jail sentence), it is best to refrain from taking a breached contract personally and instead try to collect the damages which you are entitled to recover.

The duty to mitigate damages arising from a breached contract requires the buyer and the seller to act in good faith when deciding how to obtain substitute performances or alternative supplies. The innocent seller, for example, is always required to avoid wasting a perishable good when it is commercially reasonable to resell the goods or put them in storage until another buyer can be found. If I breached an agreement to pay a fruit seller for a crate of apples, he would be under a duty to try to sell those apples elsewhere or put them in storage if that would reduce their perishability. Even though the fruit seller would rather toss the apples through the windows of my house, he will have to make sure that the apples were properly stored. Otherwise, he might be unable to claim any damages arising from their spoilage.

As suggested by the yak herder/light bulb example, the buyer is also under a duty to find alternative supplies when a seller breaches an agreement and to take whatever reasonable actions are necessary to minimize the costs of the replacement goods. The buyer cannot take some needless action that would cause him to suffer immense consequential damages (such as climbing to the yak herder's place of business, falling off the mountain, and suffering multiple injuries leading to many thousands of dollars in hospital bills) and then sue the breaching seller for those consequential damages.

The requirement that damages be mitigated also extends to employment contracts. If I fire my gardener Otto Hertz for pruning my fruit trees with a flamethrower, then he is obligated to make a good-faith effort to find another gardening job, but he is not obligated to take the first job that comes along. The obligation to reduce damages extends only to jobs that are similar to the former job in status, duties, and compensation. Even if my firing of Otto is wrongful, he must still try to find another job so as to minimize the damages that can be recovered from me. Similarly, if Otto wrongfully quits his job because he considers my attitude toward flamethrower pruning to be pigheaded, then I must make good-faith efforts to find another employee and so minimize any damages I might recover against Otto. By imposing this affirmative duty to minimize the damages of a breached employment contract, the courts have shown that they do not want former employees sitting around in their backyards all day and inflating their lost wages claims, nor do they want employers to deliberately avoid hiring replacement employees just to pump up the damages that can be obtained from the former employee. The amount of damages avoided by taking a new job or hiring a new employee is subtracted from the award received by the innocent party.

We spoke earlier of situations in which the remedy requested is not monetary damages but specific performance. In contract cases, specific performance is often requested when the item purchased is unique, such as an original painting or land. We should distinguish here between specific performance, which is a remedy in which the court orders the losing party to hand over the item in dispute, and an injunction, which is a remedy in which the court orders the losing party to refrain from doing something, such as interfering with the contractual relations of the opposing party.

A unique object may be the focus of a specific performance remedy because it has no perfect substitute on the open market and cannot be replaced by the prospective buyer. Before the specific performance remedy is given, however, the court must be satisfied that the item actually is unique and irreplaceable. If I contract to buy Leo Nardo's famous painting

"Godzilla and the Giant Praying Mantis" from the Ostentatious Art Gallery, but the gallery breaches our agreement after receiving a better offer from another party, then I could sue the gallery for specific performance of our agreement. If the court found that this painting represented the only such venture by Leo Nardo into Japanese film monster surrealism, then I would probably succeed in my request that the gallery be ordered to give me the painting in exchange for the purchase price. Specific performance would not be available if a subsequent court inquiry revealed that this painting was only one of ten million copies in existence. In such a situation, it would be unreasonable for the court to bother with the remedy of specific performance, because the vast supply of these paintings would indicate that I could easily obtain another copy of it on the open market.

Because land is considered unique, specific performance is always available for a breached real estate contract. Even though my forty-acre tract of sand in the Sahara desert might be one of 5,000 similar tracts, the courts probably would not accept my argument that a breach of my agreement to sell my property to a sandbox company would entitle the company to only nominal damages. The courts have always considered every parcel of land to be unique since there is no other property in the world having exactly the same physical features. Consequently, there can be no adequate replacement. The courts also seem to have an almost mystical attitude toward the bond between landowner and the land itself; they seem to believe that the landowner's labors, no matter how minimal, transform the land and thereby further distinguish it from any contiguous parcels.

Unlike paintings and land, the courts do not enforce personal service contracts with an order of specific performance; such a remedy would take away the employee's freedom to decide for whom to work. Moreover, the remedy of specific performance requires court supervision, and very few judges want to become bogged down in the day-to-day details of policing the performance of an unwilling worker. The court will prefer to resolve the problem at a hearing by ordering that some amount of damages be paid to the innocent party so that the two parties are then free to go their separate ways and leave the court to deal with more pressing matters, such as the judicial softball tournament.

We recall from our discussion of delegations of duties that personal service contracts may not be delegated, because they involve talents or skills that cannot be precisely duplicated by anyone else. Because the purchaser of this unique talent or skill would suffer a hardship if the delegator were permitted to delegate freely her duties to perform under the contract, the courts have found it simpler to forbid such delegations altogether. The reasoning behind this prohibition goes back to the idea that each party to a contract has certain expectation interests regarding the benefits they will derive after the contract is performed.

If I hire Flambé the Magnificent, a world-renowned swallower of flaming vacuum cleaner parts, for the evening, my motivation for entering into the contract is to provide my dinner party with the world's greatest ingester of burning appliance components. I want my guests to be impressed and overwhelmed so that they will invite me to their exclusive black-tie parties. I will not be able to make the impression I desire if Flambé the Magnificent delegates his personal service contract to Machismo the Fair-to-Middling, who makes his living setting paper on fire with a magnifying glass at children's parties. Machismo will not have the same dramatic impact as the pyrotechnically-gifted Flambé so I would be able to argue that I did not receive the benefit that I bargained for when I signed the personal services agreement with Flambé. I bargained for a performance that only Flambé could provide because I, like everybody else I know, wanted to see if he could swallow an entire vacuum cleaner. Obviously, this searing question will not be answered if Machismo shows up and starts burning holes in pieces of newspaper or upholstry.

Because specific performance is an equitable remedy that exists to promote fairness and justice, the courts have great freedom to decide when it may be used. They want to be careful that specific performance is a fair remedy under the circumstances because it is, in some ways, a more drastic remedy than a judicial order to pay money damages. If an employee of the Ostentatious Gallery mistakenly conveyed a Ming vase to a third party after I had signed a purchase agreement for the vase with the owner of the gallery, it might be extraordinarily difficult for the gallery to repurchase the item from the third party so that it could perform our contract. In such a case, the court might decide that it would be best to order the gallery to pay me the appropriate money damages so that it would not have to order the gallery to expend a huge amount of money to recover the vase.

The remedy of specific performance will not be given by the court if the party seeking specific performance has previously indicated that it would not seek such a remedy, nor will specific performance be permitted where a party has waited for an unreasonably long time before seeking the remedy, or has behaved like a skunk during the course of the transaction. There are no clear-cut rules as to when a court will deny a request for specific performance, but it is fair to say that most judges are not especially tolerant of such requests when there are any significant ambiguities in the description of the subject matter ("a red hat" versus "the red hat worn by Attila the Hun when he sacked Europe").

Another possible remedy known as recision involves the cancellation of the contract when both parties have yet to perform their duties. If the parties have exchanged consideration or promises, then the cancellation of the contract will be accompanied by the restitution (or return) of those previously conferred benefits. If I make an agreement with the Ostentatious Gallery to trade a few of my original paintings by Rubens for some sketches by unknown colorblind artists, but I soon find that the sketches are forgeries prepared by the Gallery's staff, then I could sue the gallery to have the contract cancelled and my Rubens returned to me.

The remedy of restitution is usually given when one party has somehow been "unjustly enriched." If I ordered a fifteen-foot totem pole to adorn my front yard, but it was mistakenly delivered to my next-door neighbor who refused to give it back (and stuck out her tongue at me when I pleaded for its return), my neighbor should not be permitted to retain this benefit because she is not entitled to it. In such a case, I would request the restitution of the totem pole because my neighbor had received a valuable item that was supposed to be delivered to me.

If my neighbor had promised to give me her bright orange riding lawnmower with the plow attachment (for gentlemen farmers who wish to mutilate their lawns) in exchange for my totem pole but had later welched on the deal after taking possession of my pole, then I would be entitled to sue her for the return of it because of her breach of our agreement. Of course, my behavior during this transaction would have to be acceptable or I might be prevented from getting my totem pole back. If I began tossing mangled lawn-mower pieces over the fence (the mechanical analogy to the severed ear of the kidnap victim) in the hope that my neighbor would break down and beg me to stop dismantling her beloved lawnmower, a judge might disapprove of my behavior and refuse to order that we exchange the items, even if the circumstances would have otherwise justified such a remedy.

When two people sign a contract but the writing does not accurately state the terms of the original oral agreement, the contract may be reformed by a court so that it will mirror the original agreement.

If I offered to sell two gargoyle lamps for $1,000 to an antique collector, I would be upset to find after signing the written agreement that the price of the lamps was listed as one dollar—$999 less than the amount to which we had originally agreed. Assuming that the antique collector turned a deaf ear to my plea that the correct price be inserted in the contract, I could take the matter to court and ask the judge to reform the contract so that it would correspond to our original agreement. If the judge concluded that we had originally agreed that the purchase price was $1,000, the judge would order that the correct price be inserted in the contract (and probably give a blistering lecture on business ethics to the antique collector). If, on the other hand, the collector convinced the judge that our original agreement had been for a sale price of one dollar (perhaps by using a few well-placed whines and lots of tears), then I would probably be ordered to convey the lamps for the stated price.

Situations often arise in which a contract is breached before one party has completed his performance such as when a painter stops painting a house because the owner indicates that he has no money to pay for the work. In such cases, the aggrieved party may sue for the reasonable value of the work done. If the painter had painted half the house, he might be able to obtain half of the original contract price. The amount that can be recovered will be calculated from the point of view of the painter—not the homeowner—because the painter is the one who rendered the services. Moreover, it might be more difficult to calculate the benefit of a partly painted house to the homeowner, because the uncompleted job might raise or lower the aggregate value of the house depending on the circumstances. A judge would not want to allow the breaching homeowner to say that he had obtained no benefit from the partial painting of the house or that the house was now worth less than before because of the incomplete job since then the judge might find herself ordering the painter to pay the homeowner damages for the reduced value of the house, even though the homeowner was the one who breached the agreement. In any event, there are always certain commercial standards that may be examined to determine the reasonable value of the painter's labor. It is much more difficult to determine the amount of benefit the homeowner subjectively believes he has acquired.

A variant of the idea that partial recovery should be permitted for unfinished work is found in the remedy of promissory estoppel, which we discussed previously. Promissory estoppel "arises when there is a promise which [the] promisor should reasonably expect to induce action or forbearance of a definite and substantial character on [the] part of [the] promisee, and which does induce such action or forbearance, and such promise is binding if injustice can be avoided only by enforcement of [the] promise."[1] Promissory estoppel is a remedy that may be used in many situations in which there is no formal exchange of promises or a writing evidencing an agreement. If I prom-

[1] *Black's,* 1093.

ise that I will give you my fishing boat if you rent a suitable dock slip in which to keep it, a court will not sanction my attempt to back out of the deal after you have rented the slip, because you probably would not have rented that space in the absence of my promise to give you the boat. Since it would be unjust to permit me to keep my boat after having put you in such financial difficulties, the court would order me to convey the boat to you.

In situations where a party has stated before its performance is due that it will not fulfill its contractual obligations (anticipatory repudiation) or has acted affirmatively to divest itself of the ability to perform its obligations (prospective inability to perform), the innocent party has several courses of action available to it. The innocent party can wait until the date the performance is due to see whether the opposing party will either have a change of heart or reacquire the ability to perform its part of the contract. If the situation does not change by the time the performance becomes due, the innocent party is free to pursue the standard contract remedies and thereby recover the benefit it would have received had the contract been fully performed. Even though the innocent party might be enraged by the breaching party's actions, that party will sometimes find it easier to obtain a satisfactory remedy if it waits until the date the performance is due before instituting a law suit; it may be difficult to calculate the damages due before the actual date the performance is due. However, if the breaching party seems to be suffering a financial collapse, then it may be more prudent to sue for whatever damages can be obtained instead of waiting for the date of performance to arrive when there may not be anything left to collect. One other advantage of suing immediately is that the innocent party will not have to worry about mitigating damages as would be the case if it decided to wait until the performance was due.

If I ordered a battery-powered dog from the Acme Rubber Company and received a note from them (soon after they had cashed my check) saying that they would be unable to send me my latex companion, I could wait for several weeks to see if they would change their mind (a reasonable time in the mail order business) or I could sue them immediately for the return of my money. Being the sort of person who does not want to go to court, I would probably wait to see whether the company would send me the merchandise. If two or three months passed with no indication from the company that they planned to fill the order, I would be free to sue them for the return of my money. Of course I would have to be careful not to act in a manner that might unnecessarily inflate the amount of damages that I could reasonably expect to collect or else my own recovery could be reduced accordingly. If, on the other hand, I knew that the Acme Rubber Company was beset by financial problems, I would not want to wait a commercially reasonable time for their performance. I would file a suit immediately to enhance my chances of recovering my money and also to establish my priority as a creditor should the company go bankrupt.

Chapter 5

In any transaction involving the sale of goods, the remedies available to the innocent buyer or seller depend on whether or not the goods have been accepted or not. The acceptance occurs

- when the buyer does not effectively reject the goods within a reasonable time;
- when the buyer, after a careful inspection of the goods, indicates that he will accept them despite any flaws uncovered by his inspection;
- or when the buyer acts in some way so contrary to the seller's rights of ownership that an acceptance can be presumed (such as when the buyer of cloth cuts the cloth into patterns for clothing).

A buyer may also partially accept a delivery by taking some installments and not others, but he cannot use the imperfections of one installment to avoid the entire contract unless the imperfections of an installment are great enough to impair the value of all the installments.

If the goods are delivered or otherwise made available to the buyer (tendered), then the buyer must affirmatively reject the goods within a commercially reasonable time (even if the goods do not conform with the original order), or his acceptance will be presumed. What if the defects in the goods cannot be detected by ordinary means? If the buyer accepts the goods by mistake because he was unable to detect their defects, then the buyer is not precluded from revoking his acceptance at a later date once the flaw has been uncovered. If I order a Sugar Flakes Interplanetary Space Patrol Wristwatch and accept it when it is delivered (by signing an invoice) only to find later that the item was defectively manufactured and has no secret compartment, my power to reject the item depends on whether the absence of a secret compartment is a defect that could be uncovered by reasonable inspection. If the buyer rejects the goods but fails to specify the reason for the rejection (and it is one that the seller could have remedied in a reasonable time had he been notified) then the buyer will be precluded from relying on that reason to justify his rejection of the shipment. Once the buyer rejects the goods, however, he cannot simply toss them into the street and go on his merry way. The law imposes an obligation on him (if he is not a merchant) to take care of the goods if they are in his possession. In short, he must protect the goods, but he need not take extraordinary measures to keep the goods from harm.

If I purchase a chair that is upholstered in a pink and aqua vinyl floral pattern but I reject it after it is delivered because I suddenly develop good taste, I would be under an obligation to take reasonable care of the chair while it was still in my possession. If my house caught fire that night and I barely made it outside before the roof collapsed, I would not feel particularly obligated to go back inside to fetch the chair, because it would be unreasonable for me to risk my life to prevent the chair from melting. If the chair was totally destroyed, I would have to pay for it. My rejection of it would not give me the right to incinerate it. The duty of ordinary care requires me to take reasonable steps to keep the chair from being damaged, but it does not necessitate that I take extraordinary protective measures such as building a gigantic lucite bubble in which the chair could be stored until it was reclaimed by the seller.

The Uniform Commercial Code imposes a higher duty of care on merchants than nonmerchants because those of use who do not sell goods for a living are generally ignorant about the way in which the sellers and buyers in a particular industry transact business. In any event, a merchant must not only take care of the goods, he must follow the seller's reasonable instructions as to how he should dispose of the goods. As with many other areas of contract law, there is no hard and fast definition for the word "reasonable," but it is fair to say that if you and I were steel bridge girder merchants and you delivered fifty tons of girders to me, my rejection of them would not end my duty of care. I would still have to follow your reasonable instructions for disposing of the goods. It would be reasonable for the seller to ask me to put the girders on a train and send them back to the seller; it would not be reasonable for him to expect me to mail the girders to Tibet via next-day mail. The merchant desiring to return rejected items can only ask himself if the instructions are appropriate in terms of cost, labor, and risk.

What if I am a banana merchant who orders ten cartons of bananas but instead receives ten cartons of truffles (a highly prized delicacy in the more primitive parts of France), and I am unable to contact the seller to find out how I should dispose of them? Although a nonmerchant might argue successfully that he should have no further duty of care regarding a perishable item such as truffles, I as a merchant would still be required to dispose of the goods and credit the amount received against any monies owed to me by the seller. This rule exists to prevent merchants from allowing nonconforming perishable items to rot in their warehouses; the courts want to reduce the amount of waste inherent in such shipments by requiring buyers who reject perishable goods to find alternative markets to the best of their abilities.

The remedies available to a buyer who receives nonconforming goods vary, depending on whether the buyer has already accepted the goods. If the buyer has not accepted the goods because they are defective, he may cancel the order and recover the money he paid to the seller (so that both parties are put back into their original positions), as well as any additional costs that he must incur to purchase substitutes for the goods he originally ordered on the open market. This "cover" cost is a legitimate expense. If the seller had properly performed the contract, then the buyer would not have to purchase those goods from another supplier. It is appropriate that the seller (who shipped the nonconforming goods) should bear that expense. If the item is unique, however, so that no adequate substitute is readily obtainable, then the buyer may try to obtain the item from the seller by filing a suit for specific performance (or by sneaking into his house late at night with a burlap sack).

If the seller does not fulfill the agreement and then inconveniently files for bankruptcy, the buyer may have no further recourse unless the goods were specifically identified in the contract and the buyer paid at least part of the purchase price before the seller went bankrupt. In such a situation, the buyer could pay the remainder of the purchase price and thereby compel the seller to convey the goods. The identification in the contract would operate to vest the buyer with certain rights in the goods analogous to a security interest that would defeat the seller's efforts to resell the goods to another party.

Once the buyer decides to accept the goods, he is somewhat more restricted in the way he can deal with the seller, because he has given up his unfettered power to reject the goods. If the buyer accepts a gross of table tennis balls but later finds out that each table tennis ball has a lead core, the buyer will be greatly distressed because he did not receive the goods that he ordered. Moreover, lead-filled table tennis balls are not generally accepted for regulation table tennis tournaments in most countries because they pockmark even the most durable table tennis tables and players. Although lead-filled table tennis balls may have some negligible value as holiday tree ornaments, that advantage will not mollify the buyer who desires to polish the rough edges of his table tennis game. Because the buyer has already accepted the goods, he must pay the contractual amount. However, the nonconformity of the goods gives the buyer the right to sue the seller for damages, the amount of damages being determined by the extent the value of the contract has been diminished by the breach. Because it is difficult to imagine how lead-filled table tennis balls could be used at all, the buyer should be able to recover damages equal to the purchase price of the lead-filled table tennis balls less their scrap value.

A buyer may also revoke his acceptance of nonconforming goods (which is essentially equivalent to rejecting the goods even though it occurs after the goods have been accepted) when the nonconformity of the goods is so great that it impairs the value of the goods. The buyer can revoke his acceptance if the acceptance was originally prompted by the seller swearing on a stack of Bibles that he would cure the problem and then failing to do so. Of course, the buyer must notify the seller of the defective nature of the goods within a reasonable time of the discovery, or he will be precluded from asserting a claim. To return to our lead table tennis ball example, I would have to notify the seller that I was revoking my acceptance of the shipment within a reasonable time of having discovered that the balls had solid cores. If I neglected to inform the seller for a period of months or even years, I would not be able to revoke my acceptance (even if the seller had the ability to "cure" the defect) because I did not object within a commercially reasonable time.

The seller's remedies for dealing with a buyer who breaches a contract vary depending on whether the buyer has already accepted the goods. If the buyer has not yet accepted the goods, the seller, upon learning of the buyer's unwillingness or inability to complete the transaction, can simply refuse to ship the goods to the buyer or, if they are in transit, can demand that they be returned. If the seller is making specialty goods that have no significant resale value, the seller may choose to complete the work because it would not be economical for him to stop production at that point, or he may choose to stop work because he can see no way that the costs he has already incurred can be recovered. In any event, the seller will try to recover the difference between the contract price and whatever money he is able to make by selling the item. If the transaction is one in which the item is of no value to anyone else, then the aggrieved seller might choose to sue for the contract price itself and not worry about salvaging some of the costs of the item through a resale.

Once the buyer receives and accepts the goods, the seller's remedies narrow considerably, because the seller can no longer choose to keep the goods or stop them when they are in transit. As a result, the only remedy available to the seller is a suit for the price of the goods. Although a seller may reclaim goods from an insolvent buyer (who misrepresented his financial vigor so as to obtain the goods), the seller must demand the return of the goods in a timely manner or else his claim (and his priority relative to other potential creditors) will be weakened. This situation does not pose a great problem for the seller who moonlights as a member of an elite commando unit able to recover goods wrongly retained by insolvent buyers, but for those persons who do not have recourse to such useful organizations, it is often difficult, if not impossible, to obtain the original goods or, for that matter, the full purchase price of the goods. Insolvency usually occurs when one does not have enough money to pay one's creditors. It is likely that a bankrupt buyer will not have enough money to satisfy a judgment against it for the original purchase price.

INDEX

Index

Index

Index

Index